Given in Memory of

Shirley Anderson
by
Margaret Finnerty

From LOVE FIELD

OUR FINAL HOURS WITH PRESIDENT JOHN F. KENNEDY

by

NELLIE CONNALLY
AND MICKEY HERSKOWITZ

RuggedLand

PUBLISHED BY RUGGED LAND, LLC

276 CANAL STREET · NEW YORK · NY · 10013 · USA

PUBLISHER'S CATALOGING-IN-PUBLICATION DATA

Connally, Nellie, 1919-

From love field : our final hours with president john f. kennedy /

by Nellie Connally with Mickey Herskowitz. -- 1st ed.

p. cm.

LCCN 2003108905

ISBN 1590710142

1. Kennedy, John F. (John Fitzgerald), 1917-1963—

Assassination—Personal narratives. 2. Connally, Nellie, 1919-

3. Governors' spouses—Texas—Biography.

I. Herskowitz, Mickey. II. Title.

E842.9.C66 2003 976.4'063'092

QBI03-200543

Book Design by

HSU + ASSOCIATES

RUGGED LAND WEBSITE ADDRESS: WWW.RUGGEDLAND.COM

From LOVE FIELD

RUGGED LAND : 276 CANAL STREET · NEW YORK · NY · 10013 · USA

TO JOHN

✦

Sunrises and sunsets

have never been as beautiful

as when I shared them with you.

Sleep well, my darling.

✦

From *LOVE FIELD*

Contents

ETERNITY 2

VIGIL 12

JOHN & NELLIE, JACK & JACKIE 18

I NEVER CALLED HIM LYNDON 32

LIFE AFTER DEATH 42

SECRETS AND ANXIETY 48

TEXAS HOSPITALITY 60

A BEAUTIFUL DAY IN DALLAS 70

THE SPLIT SCREEN 86

BURYING A PRESIDENT 90

JOHN, SHARON, AND MARK 96

TESTIMONY 112

COPING 124

THE DISCOVERY 130

UNSPOKEN WORDS 138

ACKNOWLEDGMENTS 205

CREDITS 207

Chapter 1

ETERNITY

We were two couples in the prime of our lives. We were two women, so proud of the men we loved. When Air Force One arrived from Fort Worth, soggy clouds still enveloped the Dallas airport. It was called Love Field. That day, November 22, 1963, the autumn air was filled with anticipation. Not everyone in Texas liked Jack Kennedy's policies, but you'd never know it from the enormous, cheering crowd that came to greet him. As if on cue, the gray clouds parted as our handsome young President

appeared at the top of the stairs. He waved to the crowd, flashing that trademark smile, and they cheered and cheered. They loved him. We all loved him.

With sunshine now around us, the bubble top to the presidential limousine seemed unnecessary. Worse, it would insult the tens of thousands who lined the streets into the city. People wanted to see their President without a barrier, with nothing between themselves and the object of so many hopes and desires. So the bubble top came off. My husband,

John Connally, the governor of Texas, and I followed Jack and Jackie down the stairs. At the bottom of the steps, befitting that beautiful morning, Jackie accepted a bouquet of glistening roses—all red, a complement to her pink suit. I received another, but my roses were yellow. What other flower could the wife of a Texas governor carry?

The Secret Service tried to hurry us into the car, but Jack and Jackie insisted on "working the crowd." They strolled along the chain-link fence surrounding the tarmac, shaking hands and smiling and chatting with any and all in their calm, gracious way. It made the Secret Service men nervous.

Eventually, we climbed into the long, black Lincoln. Our driver, Agent William Greer, looked relieved, as did the agent riding shotgun, Roy Kellerman. He spoke into his lapel: "We are leaving Love Field."

Jack and Jackie sat on the upholstered bench in the back, slightly raised so that people could see them better. John and I took the two jump seats between the back bench and the front, where our driver and security man were already in place. As we rolled forward, John pivoted and spoke briefly with the President in that easygoing, expansive way I had come to love. The President looked pleased. Jackie was as relaxed as I had ever seen her.

More than anything, I'd hoped Dallas—a conservative stronghold—would give the Kennedys a warm and friendly welcome. With great pride, I beamed at our guests, at my husband, at our eager Texans cheering and waving, and knew that things could not be better.

Our caravan gathered speed and passed through downtown Dallas. It was scheduled to end at a local landmark known as the triple underpass, just beyond an old brick building called the Texas School Book Depository. Built in 1901, the facade had been sandblasted over the years to the color of red dust. It originally housed offices for the Southern Rock Island Plow Company. Sooner than we could know, it would join Ford's Theatre as a dark shrine in American history.

The Kennedys acknowledged the adoring crowd, the breeze stirring Jack's boyish hair above that familiar Irish grin. Jackie, serene in a pink suit, with her red roses, glanced blissfully at her admirers.

The Texas sun warms quickly, and her hand reached for a pair of sunglasses. The President looked at her, cocked his head, and said, "Take off your glasses, Jackie."

Obediently, she returned them to her purse.

We followed Elm Street toward Stemmons Freeway, heading for the Trade Mart, where the President was to deliver his third speech of the day. The School Book Depository slipped by on our right and the shadow of the underpass approached—we were almost at the end of our journey.

We were indeed a happy foursome that beautiful morning. I had my yellow roses in my arms and Jackie had her red roses in hers. The crowds were the largest and the friendliest we had had on the trip thus far. I did so hope Dallas would give the Kennedys a warm and very cordial welcome, and I wanted the Kennedys to respond with equal warmth and friendliness. I could not have been more pleased. I felt tingly all over with the pride of a mother whose children are performing in front of the relatives just as she had hoped.

We had pleasant banter back and forth among the four of us, but mostly the Kennedys were responding to a rousing ovation, and John and I were just smiling with genuine pleasure that everything was so perfect. We had passed through the downtown area and its great, surging, happy, friendly crowds.

I was so excited; I turned to the President and said, "Mr. President, you certainly can't say that Dallas doesn't love you!" His eyes met mine and his smile got even wider. Dallas had surprised him.

I turned back toward the driver. A moment later, a terrifying noise erupted behind us. Instinctively, I felt it was a gunshot.

I looked back and saw the President's hands fly up to his throat. He made no sound, no cry—nothing. His expression hadn't changed—no grimace, no sign of pain. But the eyes—those eyes were full of surprise.

At that instant, I was shocked and confused. I had a

horrifying feeling that the President not only had been shot, but could be dead.

From the corner of my eye, I saw my husband, John, turn clockwise in his seat. But the car door prevented him from seeing clearly, so he twisted the other way, toward me. He had been in the war. He was a hunter. He knew the sound of gunshots.

"No, no, no!" he cried out.

Then—a second shot.

My husband spun in his seat. He had been hit in the back by the second bullet. "My God," he blurted, "they are going to kill us all!" —then crumpled forward.

All I thought was, *What can I do to help John?* I pulled him into my lap. I didn't want him hurt any more.

A third shot rang out.

I felt something falling all over us. I looked up. Tiny bits of bloody matter covered my suit, the car, everything. I no longer had any doubt that the President was dead. I looked down. John was bleeding badly all over the front of his shirt. He was not moving.

I had one arm under his head, the other across his chest. I thought my husband was dead.

"Jack—Jack!"

From the backseat, I heard Jackie's frantic voice.

"They've killed my husband! I have his brains in my hand!"

I hugged John tighter. More blood gushed from his shirt.

Dimly, I heard one of the agents shout, "Pull out of the motorcade"—then say something else into his transmitter, probably to the motorcycle officers ahead and to the vehicle full of Secret Service men behind us—"to the nearest hospital."

The big Lincoln, long and black as a hearse, swerved out of formation and accelerated at tremendous speed. Maybe it was in reaction to the surging car, but John finally stirred in my arms. I felt tremendous relief—as if we had both been reborn. I pulled his right arm over his chest in order to hold him closer.

"Shhh. Be still. It's all right. Be still. It's all right."

I repeated this mantra until the big car braked at the emergency room entrance to Parkland Memorial Hospital. I had no idea how long the trip had taken. The people along our route were just a blur of color. Their cheers had become the wind roaring all around us. For an instant, I felt an overwhelming sense of pity: that on this beautiful day, when they had come out to see their President and his First Lady, they found instead two terrified women holding their dying husbands in their arms.

As soon as the car stopped, the doors swung open and a dozen people swarmed over us. Secret Service men were everywhere. They were crying, "Mr. President," and were pleading with Mrs. Kennedy to get out of the car.

Mrs. Kennedy, you've got to get out!

Apparently Jackie, still in shock, wasn't about to abandon her husband. The Secret Service agents tried to pry her from the President's body.

How long must I wait before I could call for help?

After what seemed like forever, John heaved himself out of my arms and fell heavily toward the door. Thinking quickly, Dave Powers, a member of the White House staff, picked him up in his arms like a baby and gently placed him on a stretcher. They ran off down the strange corridor with him and I ran along behind the stretcher.

"It hurts—"

I heard John's voice, and I knew he was still alive.

Just as quickly, the stretcher disappeared into Trauma Room Two. The door slammed in my face.

I had never felt so alone.

There was pandemonium in the halls, guns everywhere. The federal agents had tommy guns and automatic rifles. The Dallas police had their handguns drawn, unsure of the scope of the plot that they feared was unfolding.

A few minutes before they brought in the body of the President, a Secret Service agent burst into the trauma room, waving a submachine gun. Everyone in the room hit the floor.

A man in a dark business suit ran in after him. The agent knocked him out with one punch, and as the man slid down the wall, he reached into his coat pocket and pulled out an FBI badge.

A second later, a gurney bearing the President, surrounded by an emergency room team, rattled past and disappeared into Trauma Room One, right across from John's. That door, too, slammed shut. Like me, another woman in a pink suit, also splattered with her husband's blood, stood forlornly in the hall. ✦

Chapter 2

....

VIGIL

he agents and police quickly secured the building—clearing out nonessential people. They found one Dallas reporter hiding under a sheet in the ER—I never found out what happened to him. They even posted guards by the pay telephones, worried that someone might tip the press—or, worse, call in more assassins.

Amid all the confusion, some thoughtful person brought two straightbacked chairs for Jackie and me to sit on and put them in the hallway. I sat immediately, before my legs could buckle.

For an instant, Jackie and I stared at each other across the emotional gulf between us. For all we knew, my husband was still alive; but the chances for hers, at best, were grim. People in the hallway ran crazily between us. Neither of us cried; our eyes weren't even wet.

Time passed. We may have sat in those chairs for a few minutes or an hour or all day—we didn't know.

Intuition told me from the moment I saw Jack Kennedy grab his throat that our thirty-fifth President was dead. I think Jackie Kennedy knew it too. They took her into Trauma Room One just as the white sheet was pulled over her husband's handsome face. I was told a priest, Father Oscar Huber, was already there. He had given Jack the last rites and told Jackie that the President's soul, he believed, had still been in the body at that time. It would comfort her to know the final sacrament had not only been delivered, but received.

More than fifteen doctors and nurses had attended the late President. None of them wanted to say the obvious: The President was dead. Eventually, when it was clear to even the most stubborn of them that there was nothing more to be done, they said what had to be said.

A few minutes later, in the nurses' lounge one floor above, at the other end of the hospital where reporters had been corralled, White House spokesman Malcolm Kilduff announced in a voice thick with emotion, "President John Fitzgerald Kennedy died at approximately one o'clock."

Slowly, the pieces of this awful tragedy began to take their shape.

Jack Kennedy had been seriously wounded by the first shot—the first shot I'd heard from my seat in front of Jackie—and was killed by the third. The second bullet entered my husband's back, shattered his ribs, and blew out of his chest, sending splinters of bone into one lung. It penetrated his right wrist and came to rest in his left leg, where it stayed lodged until surgeons removed it. In Trauma Two, as doctors examined his wounds, they assumed John was unconscious and did not sedate him. They probed and prodded, squeezed and pressed as if my husband could feel no pain. Tracing the zigzag pattern of hideous wounds, the emergency room physician, Dr. Tom Shires, asked those in attendance, "How many times was he shot?"

John answered, "Once." The doctors jumped.

They tried next to remove his trousers, but caused so much pain that John finally told them, "Cut the damn things off!" then passed out. Blood covered his whole body—it was easy to understand why the doctors had so much trouble assessing his wounds. Even his forehead was sprayed with blood. For many minutes they scoured his head for another wound, then realized the blood and matter belonged to Jack Kennedy.

That John survived his wounds was incredible. That he survived his examination was a miracle—or so I thought at the time. Later, I discovered I needn't have worried.

A talented young doctor, James "Red" Duke—the first physician to reach him—would later become chief of surgery at the University of Texas Medical School. He was, in fact, a protégé of Dr. Robert Shaw, a famous surgeon who had just returned from Afghanistan and was, at that moment, being airlifted by NASA from Houston just to operate on my husband.

With John in the hands of the doctors, my thoughts now turned to our three children: seventeen-year-old John III, our oldest; our fourteen-year-old daughter, Sharon; and eleven-year-old Mark—our youngest, still in grade school. I wanted to tell them what had happened as soon as possible, but what on earth would I say?

I asked someone to call Austin, where the children attended three different schools. I wanted the principals to tell them that their father was alive, that was the main thing. Who knew what the radio and TV were saying? The assassination of a President—and the ascension of a new leader—left little time or space in the news for a wounded governor. In fact, reports about John Connally—when he was mentioned at all—were either conflicting or erroneous. One report said both the President and the Governor had been killed; that was obviously wrong. Another said the Vice President, Lyndon Johnson, had suffered a heart attack—a report based, apparently, on someone seeing Johnson (who did have a massive coronary in 1955) come into the hospital holding his right arm over his chest—also untrue—though our old friend was definitely in another kind of pain. Another report told of three wounds in my husband's head. Yet another said he'd been shot several times in the chest. And so it went. These were the reports I feared our children were hearing, and I ached to tell them the truth.

But my job just then was keeping my vigil, just as Jackie had kept hers.

At one point, a receptionist asked me to come to the office and fill out an admitting form for John Connally. I did not move.

After another endless stretch of time, Earl Cabell, the mayor of Dallas, appeared beside my chair.

"Is there anything I can do for you, Nellie?" he asked quietly.

I thanked him, and said no. But it was nice to know I had a friend at this unbelievable time.

Bill Stinson, my husband's travel aide, had been riding a few cars behind us in the motorcade. He made it to the hospital almost as fast as the Secret Service and had accompanied John into Trauma. Now its terrible door creaked open and a masked nurse peeked out. Behind her I saw John, deathly pale on the examining table—but clearly alive: I heard a moan and saw a twitching foot.

The nurse dropped one of John's gold cuff links, made with a Mexican peso, into my hand. The other had been shot off. Bill came out right after that and said, "The Governor just told me, please go take care of Nellie."

I felt another lump in my throat. That was John Connally. Shot to pieces, his fate measured in heartbeats—and his main concern was for me.

I've thought back on that moment often. It sustained me through the most terrible time in my life. It sustains me to this day and could, if necessary, sustain me forever. ✦

Chapter 3

JOHN & NELLIE, JACK & JACKIE

*A*s a couple, John and I had crossed paths with Jack and Jackie only rarely before that fateful drive from Love Field.

The first time was when John F. Kennedy, a freshman senator from Massachusetts, attended the Democratic National Convention in Chicago during August 1956. John and Jack had two similar functions to perform, but for totally different people. John delivered a rousing speech nominating Lyndon Johnson for President. Jack nominated Adlai Stevenson.

In those days, Texas senator Johnson and Illinois governor Stevenson represented opposite poles of the Democratic Party. Johnson was tough, earthy, and master of the muddy trenches of political warfare. Stevenson was cerebral, articulate, and gave the impression that he was somehow above the fray. They were the yin and yang of American politics, and it was clear from the start which of these larger-than-life characters Jack Kennedy most admired.

John and Jack almost knocked each other over at the convention, one climbing onto the podium, the other descending. I don't think they said a word to each other all evening. In those days, politics was a bare-knuckles brawl for power, and national conventions were still places where anything could happen. Although they later became good friends and political allies, that night Jack and John were opponents and behaved accordingly. The stakes were very high.

John told me Lyndon Johnson wasn't really interested in being President, at least in 1956. He wanted to orchestrate the convention, and to do that he needed to position himself as something more than another "favorite son"—one of the endless stream of state politicians nominated, then discarded, when the powerbrokers began to haggle. In those days, delegates were fickle and excitable. Master politicians like Johnson knew how to manipulate them: Create a slate of potential contenders, then sweep it clean with a last-minute compromise—usually, the candidate Johnson had in mind all along.

John went along with all this even though he was one of the few who no longer believed in this tradition. Most of the Texas delegation hoped that somehow the convention could be stampeded into dumping Stevenson—who had lost badly to Eisenhower in '52—and run someone with a better chance, possibly from Texas.

The demonstration after John's nominating speech was surprisingly loud and raucous. The network commentators—still figuring out how to cover such events on TV—wondered aloud if their cameras hadn't missed something. They had: the skillful manipulation of state delegates by Sam Rayburn, then Speaker of the House, arguably the most powerful man in Congress. Nobody dared to offend "Mister Sam," so every state paraded noisily under the LBJ banner.

Of course, Stevenson won easily on the first ballot. The real contest was to come: the fight for second place on the ticket—the target Johnson had in his sights from the beginning.

The two leading prospects were Jack Kennedy, a rising star from Massachusetts, and Estes Kefauver of Tennessee, a setting sun in democratic politics but a man who still commanded national attention. For the first time in history, Stevenson opened the vice presidential nomination to the floor—a move that shocked everyone, including Lyndon Johnson and John Connally.

Seeing the handwriting on the wall, Johnson quickly endorsed Kennedy, who was also Rayburn's choice. Then Johnson got a Mexican-American delegate from the Rio Grande Valley to make a moving speech on Kennedy's behalf. It was a favor that Johnson would hope to collect on later.

Lyndon Johnson enjoyed wielding power, but he liked being a kingmaker more. Johnson saw great potential in Jack

Kennedy, and genuinely liked the gangly Ivy Leaguer as well—though the affection wasn't always returned. Johnson didn't think much of Kefauver, who was best known as chairman of an antiracketeering committee. Kefauver fancied himself a modern-day Davy Crockett and loved posing for pictures in a coonskin cap.

But the Kennedy plan failed and Kefauver won his place on the ticket. It was just as well. Kefauver and Stevenson were buried in the second Eisenhower landslide, turning Stevenson into the kind of martyr Democrats love: a man too nice to win—a lesson not lost on Jack Kennedy, who made Stevenson his representative to the U.N.

By 1960, Jack Kennedy had a machine of his own. He came to the national convention in Los Angeles—the first Roman Catholic with a real chance of winning the presidency—with many of the delegates locked up: the first in a new type of convention. Lyndon Johnson also viewed 1960 as his year, but his efforts were halfhearted. John Connally managed his campaign, and LBJ was backed by all the party elders, including Adlai Stevenson and Eleanor Roosevelt. But Johnson started too late with too little. So Kennedy won the Democratic nomination.

Against the wishes of his own brother Bobby, Kennedy chose Johnson as his running mate. It was the wisest political decision he ever made. John and all of LBJ's supporters worked hard to make sure they carried Texas. The margin was tight, but they did. And that made the difference in the national election. Without carrying Texas, Kennedy never would have become President.

After the election, to reward John (or maybe just to keep him within arm's reach in Washington), Johnson asked the new President to appoint my husband Secretary of the Navy.

"Why would he want it?" Kennedy asked, apparently surprised.

"He was a Navy man in the war," Johnson answered. "He loves the Navy."

So did the young President, whose adventures on *PT-109*—the torpedo boat that was rammed by a Japanese destroyer in World War II—helped create his legend.

So the Connallys spent 1961 in the nation's capital. We could've stayed longer, but one of John's great strengths was to recognize when he had done all he could in a particular job, then move on. It took him a year to overhaul what he could in our new nuclear-powered Navy, and Washington was never our kind of town.

We socialized when we had to, and occasionally with the Kennedys, but we didn't know them well. Jack Kennedy was always cordial, and John considered him a friend—someone whose wit and self-confidence he greatly admired. For his part, Jack Kennedy was a practical guy, someone John knew he could argue with and not face recriminations. That trait produced a lot of loyal followers across political lines.

I thought I knew what "charisma" meant before I met Jack Kennedy, but our young President gave the word a new definition. He was masculine and boyish at the same time—a neat trick and a powerful combination. He had a mischievous, even flirtatious twinkle in his eye that drove women crazy. We heard rumors about his extracurricular activities, but frankly those stories never interested me. I had a handsome husband of my own to worry about, and Washington was filled with predatory women looking for a fling with a famous man. I thought, Nellie, you've got to do something. You need a plan. You can't go around scratching other women's eyes out!

Believe it or not, I took my lead from John himself. A man hasn't been born who doesn't like to be admired by women, and John was no exception. Politics is a pressure cooker and Washington is the center of the stove. I figured that John could blow off as much steam as he liked during the day—flirt, smile, enjoy the attention of a hundred fancy (and often very young and beautiful) women—but as long as he came home to me and the kids at night, our marriage would prevail. And it did.

I don't think Jackie was as lucky.

She was what we in Texas called "a man's woman." She didn't seem to crave the company of other females. I first suspected this when I met a fashionable young lady at a Washington reception. We talked about this and that, then she went into a long discussion about Jackie's taste in clothing,

art, and furniture. It sounded like she knew her well.

"Are you and Mrs. Kennedy friends?" I asked, impressed with her insider knowledge.

"I was in their wedding."

"You were?" I was astonished.

"Yes." She then went on matter-of-factly, "And I haven't seen or spoken to her since."

There had been no fight, no breakup, no hard feelings between them. That was simply Jackie. It left me with a very different view of the charming, gracious First Lady I had come to know—the one who always seemed so approachable, yet to others, so aloof.

I learned more about Jackie during a boat trip on the Potomac. As I said, Jack and John were old Navy men, so their tastes both turned toward sailing. As Secretary of the Navy, John had access to two presidential yachts kept in immaculate condition. The *Sequoia* had been in service since the days of Herbert Hoover. Jack Kennedy had taken a fancy to another ship, the *Lenore,* and renamed it the *Honey Fitz,* after his grandfather, John Fitzgerald, the legendary mayor of Boston.

But this evening, the party was embarked on two large yachts. The President boarded the first with a handful of dignitaries; the First Lady boarded ours, hostess to the rest of us. John escorted Jackie up the gangway, past the usual garland of roses, and a white-jacketed Navy officer showed them to their seats. I followed, two steps behind: the customary position for spouses with no particular ceremonial role.

John and Jackie obviously enjoyed each other's company—he was animated and charming as ever, and Jackie warm and regal. I remember telling myself, *Good night, Nellie—your evening is over!* But I wasn't jealous. I imagined our commander-in-chief dazzling the women on the first boat just as Jackie was commandeering all male hearts on the second. I never doubted her devotion to Jack. She simply preferred the company of men.

In truth, John and I always though Jack and Jackie made a perfect couple. Two puzzle pieces fit together not because they are the same, but because they are different, and complement each another. The Kennedy children—Caroline and John-John—were adorable. On the night Jack Kennedy was elected, John and I felt personally blessed. It was a great victory not just for our party but for the nation. We needed a young and vigorous leader after the string of presidents who preceded him. The fifties was a time of consolidation and building. Now we needed to release some of that raw energy—and our handsome young First Family were the perfect icons to show us how.

But life inside the Beltway wasn't really our cup of tea. When John accepted the Navy post, one of the first things he asked was whether we had to join the famous "five parties a night" social circuit. Kennedy's people told him we were obliged to attend only those events involving the Navy—and, of course, the White House itself—so that's exactly what we did.

At my first official Navy luncheon, I was asked to give a short talk. I was nervous, as you'd expect, but I had heard enough of my husband's speeches to know what to say, and how—so far as I was able. I thought I'd made a mess of things, until I was swamped the following week with letters telling me I'd made the annual luncheon the best it had been in years. I could only wonder how dull their previous events had been!

I was invited to christen a new Polaris submarine about to be launched at Newport News, Virginia: the *USS Sam Houston*. The Texan connection was obvious since it was the namesake of the first president of the Texas Republic.

Of course, I was delighted, but felt I should clear it first with John, whom I suspected was behind the whole thing. He only laughed and said he had nothing to do with it, though he was happy to sign the necessary letter authorizing my visit.

On my way to the naval yard, I kept thinking about the old Movietone newsreels I'd seen as a girl—the ones showing nervous wives in big white hats trying to break a bottle of champagne across the bow. It didn't look easy, and I was sure I'd mess it up.

My assistant that day was Janie Briscoe, a wonderful young woman from Texas. She was supposed to help me out and tell me what to do, but I honestly think she was more nervous than I was.

I knew Navy superstition held that if you didn't break the bottle, the ship would have back luck.

We mounted the platform with the official party, and, after the preliminaries, I grabbed the neck of the bottle and swung it as hard as I could.

Nothing. It didn't break.

Even worse, the ship began sliding down the ways.

Panicked, I leaned out and gave it another whack, this time hitting the steel just above my hands. As it turns out, that is the "sweet spot" for christening ships: the weakest part of the bottle. Elated, I watched the frothy foam splash everywhere. The crowd cheered and I cheered with them— not in triumph, but relief. I told Janie later that if that second swing had failed, I was grabbing the bow with one hand and going down with the ship—and grabbing her with the other because she was going down with me!

All in all, our year in Washington passed quickly. We saw the Kennedys on occasion and our relationship deepened— and I believe we became casual friends. After we returned to Texas, John ran for governor and was elected, which made him an important ally for the new President and a pivotal player—and sometimes bridge—for the master tactician who was now his Vice President: Lyndon Baines Johnson. ✦

Chapter 4

I NEVER CALLED HIM LYNDON

✦

It seemed as if I had been in the corridor at Parkland Hospital half my life when a kind administrator (or someone in authority) showed me to a private waiting room.

My room was no bigger than a prison cell: very plain, with a couple of chairs, a window, a table with some magazines—old issues of *The Saturday Evening Post* and *Life*, plus the day's Dallas newspaper, which someone had already

read and tried vainly to reassemble. I never even glanced at it, afraid to see a headline touting—or criticizing—our fallen president's Texas visit.

I now realized that Lyndon Johnson, another famous son of Texas, was about to become our next President. I felt sorry for him—real anguish. I knew he wanted to be President, but this was the last way he'd want to gain office: catapulted into the White House over the body of his President.

We first met the Johnsons shortly after John graduated from the University of Texas and took a job as LBJ's congressional aide. John rose quickly in the ranks of staffers and ran several of Johnson's campaigns, including his unsuccessful bid to win the 1960 presidential nomination.

Johnson was more than a boss and mentor to my husband: He was John's "big brother." I was amazed when I first heard about—then witnessed—one of their famous shouting matches. Johnson would call John, or John would call Johnson, and they would begin talking about some plan or policy or political deal they had cooking. Gradually, John's voice would rise, then one or the other would slam down the receiver. Sometimes, they went for weeks without speaking to each other—just exchanging terse notes or communicating through intermediaries. But in the end, they always got back together. And nobody was fiercer defending Johnson's name or interests than his loyal campaign manager. John's attitude about the whole thing was, *He's my brother. I can punch him but don't you touch him.*

I knew Lyndon Johnson in my own right. I had worked for a committee to raise money for congressional races, and LBJ was its head. I was willing to do anything useful, which wasn't much since I didn't type, couldn't take dictation, and didn't know a file drawer from a nail file. My forte was answering phones—any Texas teenager can do that, I thought—and got pretty good at it. I deflected prying journalists and spying Republicans; made all our donors, big or small, feel important; and kept our boss connected with the outside world. Arm twisting and cajoling were his stock-in-trade, of course, and my phone line was his umbilical cord.

Except once.

A call came in from a major contributor in California, and Johnson was working him well, when I accidentally broke the connection. I didn't even know I had done it until I felt the breeze from a heavy object sail past my head, stirring my hair. A book thudded against the wall. He didn't cuss me out—though he was capable of that—and I learned his aim with blunt objects was too good and well practiced to miss except on purpose. Half of politics is intimidation, they say, and that day LBJ planted his "brand" solidly on my slowly thickening hide.

I never disconnected a call again, and always called him by his title—Congressman, Senator, Vice President—or Mr. Johnson, and never Lyndon, even after John became governor.

Never.

LBJ was a hard man to like but an easy man to admire. Many even loved him. And the devotion of his staffers was legend, and completely understandable. In the end, I would have forgiven him anything because of the kindness he showed my husband, and the real interest he took in his career.

Lady Bird, Johnson's wife, was completely different. (Like I say, political marriages often attract opposites.) She was warm and pleasant, with none of Jackie's aristocratic aura. If Johnson was John's "big brother," Lady Bird was my big sister. When her husband and mine were off to war, we tried our best to run the congressman's office. Lady Bird knew shorthand, not well, and decided to take a refresher course. She invited me to join her.

After the first week, Lady Bird and I were assigned to different classes. After the second, I dropped out. Part of my decision was aptitude, I suppose, but I think the real reason I sabotaged my own stenographic career was that I couldn't bear the thought of working knee-to-knee with the man who had almost brained me, and made a habit of yelling at John.

One day, Lady Bird asked, "Nellie, your instructor asked me, 'Whatever happened to that pretty young lady who came with you to the first class?' I didn't know what to tell him. Have you stopped taking classes?"

I answered yes, but didn't tell her the reason. Knowing Lady Bird—and knowing how well she knew her own husband—I didn't think I had to. She just nodded, sympathetic as always, and gave me a big hug. I did not want to take dictation from the two men in our lives—day or night—just because I could!

Now Lady Bird was in the doorway of my hospital waiting room. She had already seen Jackie and was leaving for the airport, where, in a matter of hours, she would replace her as First Lady. She opened her arms wide and I flew into them, and I cried and cried for the first time.

Until that moment, until Lady Bird arrived, I didn't have time to cry. Now it was okay. That was the effect she had, and the kind of woman she was.

"Nellie," she said softly in that precise, lilting Texas accent of hers, "I'd like to stay. But they want Lyndon back in Washington as soon as possible."

I said I understood and hugged her extra hard. She would need all her strength—and more, as we all would—over the coming days and months.

It was now midafternoon on the longest day of my life. Foot traffic in the hospital hallway slowly began to thin. The Secret Service called a Dallas funeral home and asked them to send over the best casket they had in stock. The owner already knew what the Secret Service man said next, "It's for the President of the United States."

Jackie left the hospital with her husband in the coffin.

Before Air Force One could depart Love Field, however, federal district Judge Sarah Hughes, a Kennedy appointee and

a friend of the Johnson family, boarded the plane to swear in the thirty-sixth President of the United States. In contrast to the gala festivities of the weeklong Kennedy inauguration, the new president's ceremony lasted two minutes.

Shortly thereafter, Air Force One lifted off, the body of its fallen leader safely ensconced in the small bedroom at the rear of the plane. Thirty minutes out of Washington, I received a call from our new chief executive, my old boss.

"We are praying for you, darling," Lyndon Johnson said. "I know everything is going to be all right, isn't it? Give him a hug and kiss for me."

As soon as I was able—as soon as the doctors and nurses

and Secret Service agents and policemen and administrators would let me—that's exactly what I would do. ✦

Chapter 5

LIFE AFTER DEATH

After an endless wait, a mass of medical people—doctors, nurses, and orderlies swarming like flies around the gurney—wheeled my husband out of the emergency room and toward the operating room. I caught only the quickest glimpse of John—face covered with an oxygen mask, body hidden by a thin drape trailing fluid-filled plastic tubes.

Again I ran after them, down one strange corridor after another, only to be shut out at the end of the trail. Again I consigned myself to the purgatory of the waiting room.

This time I didn't have long to wait. Dr. Shaw, the famous thoracic surgeon and a kind and dedicated man, came out and explained the nature of John's wounds and what they were preparing to do about them. He said Bill Stinson would be allowed in the operating room to bring bulletins to me during what figured to be a long operation.

The good news, Dr. Shaw said, was that the bullet had somehow missed his major arteries. This, despite the fact that the exit wound in John's chest was the size of a baseball. He praised me for having the presence of mind to move John's right arm over his chest on the way to the hospital. He told me it was an old trick used on the battlefield when a soldier gets a sucking chest wound. Unless it's closed immediately, the victim will likely die. Medics are trained to stuff anything—a handkerchief, a torn shirt, a sock—into the wound to shut off the flow of air. I, of course, knew nothing of that. Pulling John as close as possible was pure instinct, the way a mother holds an injured child. Even if I'd known to stuff something into his ghastly chest wound, I would've fainted if I tried.

Hope, now, gradually replaced the adrenaline that was holding me up. Bill's bulletins kept me apprised of every grisly detail: The pierced lung was being repaired; the fractured fifth rib would regenerate its five missing inches over time. Because of John's strong constitution and determination to live, the prognosis was guarded, but positive.

Family and friends arrived at the hospital while John was in surgery. Seventeen-year-old John III was the first to arrive, and was I glad to see him and have him with me. Later, he said, "Dad had impressed on us that Mom was always alone when we had a crisis. I wanted to be with her and I wanted to be close to my dad. So, even with Mother saying wait—I went."

My sister, Sheba, and her husband, Bill Bryant, arrived, coming from nearby Sherman. John's brother, Merrill Connally, and his wife, Mary, followed soon thereafter. Although they wore the mask of shock that had become the uniform of the day, just seeing their faces gave me an immediate lift. Before long we had a genuine support group: John's mother, Lela, and his sister, Blanche; our good friends Adele Locke, the Cassidys and Strausses from Dallas, and Judge John Singleton, from Houston.

As soon as I knew John would live, I called our children, now safely in the arms—and under the watchful eye—of my mother, Katie Brill, at the governor's mansion in Austin.

According to the school administrators, our sons and daughter had been exceptionally brave. Officers from the Texas Department of Public Safety, assigned to the governor's mansion, picked them up and brought them home, where they stayed by the phone, monitoring the radio and TV, until I could call.

Of course, they all wanted to come to Dallas, but I said we would save that trip until later—hopefully, not too far into the future—when their daddy would be awake and able to speak. Sharon and Mark agreed, but John III arranged for a plane by calling the director of the Department of Public Safety and arrived in Dallas while his father was still in recovery. I should've been put out for his failure to "follow mother's orders," but I was secretly relieved to see him. He remained at Parkland most of the time I was there, a pillar of support I now know I would've sorely missed. In that way, too, he is very much like his father.

The surgery ended at 5:23 P.M. They took my husband to the recovery room, a large L-shaped ward with a half dozen beds. I was shown to another little cell—this time with no window—but it had one luxury the other lacked: It opened directly onto the recovery room. I could now walk out and see John whenever I felt the need. Over the next few hours, I would feel very needy indeed.

One of the doctors came to my little cell and said I could finally visit my husband. "He's going to make it," he said with a weary grin, and I felt my knees would buckle. I immediately went with him to the recovery room.

My first look at John was a terrible shock—almost as bad as that horrible, endless ride to Parkland after the shooting. Tubes ran from every part of his body: right leg, left arm, and from the front and back of his chest. His wounded arm hung in a sling and an oxygen mask covered his face. Although the doctor assured me, *He's going to make it,* it was clear there were plenty of things that might still go wrong.

I crossed the floor and leaned lightly against the bed, afraid I would fall if I stood unassisted. My first task was to fulfill the solemn promise I had made to myself and to the new President and his First Lady. I leaned over and kissed him softly.

That was a defining moment for John and me. We had been through so much and had been spared. We still had each other and could go on and fulfill whatever mission fate had in store for us. We knew for this one precious moment how lucky we were.

I thought I saw John smile through his mask despite his pain and numbing effect of his medications. One of the first things he said was "This is—" and introduced me to his nurse. My husband, the ultimate gentleman!

Later on, as John's head cleared, he was able to communicate better. He asked about President Kennedy, whom he remembered seeing wounded. I evaded the question and consulted his doctors, who decided it would be better to break the news to him later, when he was stronger.

On Saturday morning, when he asked about Kennedy again, I answered, "The President is dead."

"I knew . . ." His voice, soft and sad, just trailed off.

The next few days were long, and most of the nights sleepless. When I was finally able to stop the replay of that terrible day in my mind and fall asleep, it appeared again in my dreams. All everyone talked about was the assassination: what had happened and why. That was the worst question: *Why?* Part of me was afraid we would never find an answer. Part of me was afraid that we would. ✶

Chapter 6

:::

SECRETS AND ANXIETY

J finally asked for a sleeping pill and got some rest. I didn't usually take pills, but I had been able to doze off for only an hour or two.

Ever since our arrival, the hospital had been under tight security. There was a guard outside my door and two guards at all times in the recovery room. I didn't see much of the building, but wherever we went and wherever we looked there were uniformed police and agents. The crime may have

THE DALLAS TIMES HERALD

CONTINUOUSLY PUBLISHED FOR 87 YEARS   THE TIMES 1876   THE HERALD 1886   CONSOLIDATED 1888

87th Year—No. 292   DALLAS, TEXAS, FRIDAY EVENING, NOVEMBER 22, 1963   Telephones—Cross-Rd. RM 1414   3 Parts   Price Five

FINAL
EDITION

— Suspect Arrested —

PRESIDENT DEAD
CONNALLY SHOT

Johnson

been committed, but the danger—and the anxiety—was far from over.

One reason was that the dimensions of the assassination were yet unknown. Already, conspiracy theories ran wild. Many of them were fueled by John's exclamation at the time he was hit: *My God, they're going to kill us all!* Who was this mysterious *they* and how did the governor of Texas know about them? Even Lyndon Johnson was accused by some of being part of a plot hatched by right-wing Texas oilmen.

Of course, the meaning of my husband's exclamation was clear enough to me. John had been in the war, and military men, like politicians, think of people in groups, their minds work *in the plural.* "They" are the enemy. "They" are our friends. All he knew was, at the instant he was hit, his wife and friends were under attack. "They" could—and probably would—kill all of us unless something happened. Fortunately for myself and Jackie, something did. Unfortunately for our husbands, our escape came seconds too late.

Our security men continued to rethink their arrangements. Some wanted to move John immediately to a private room, which was less accessible than where he was. I objected, saying that as long as he needed the suction tubes and electric paddles and all the other specialized gear they kept in the recovery room, that's where he would stay. In the end, my argument won—with support from our marvelous doctors.

By then I was convinced that John had received the best medical care possible, let alone at Parkland. One naturally assumes the A-list doctors and nurses will swarm to a President's bedside; but from the time Jack was brought in, there was very little doubt in anyone's mind—certainly not in mine or Jackie's—that there was only one trauma patient to be saved on that terrible day. And the rest of the hospital staff were as wonderful as the doctors and nurses. Everyone was good to us. Flowers, telegrams, and letters poured in. A small governor's office was even set up so that he could get back to work as soon as his phone arm, brain, and energy were up to the task.

I had spent all Friday, November 22, in my pink suit, blood-streaked and rumpled. I'd packed a few things for the presidential trip to Dallas—three suits and a cocktail dress—but I was unprepared for a longer stay, and certainly not for the business at hand.

Adele Locke brought me some of her clothes—a couple of day dresses, a robe, nightgowns, and shoes. They were necessary—I wore them all and I loved her for her thoughtfulness.

After John moved to the recovery room, my life settled into a kind of routine, if that word can be used for those hectic, tumultuous days. I tried to keep "normal" hours. I got up and got dressed, ate and slept and read mail, made and received phone calls, and kept an ear on the radio and an eye on the TV, like everybody else in our shocked and sorrowful nation.

It also gave me a chance to catch up on what had been happening with the other important people in my life.

My sister-in-law, Merrill Connally's wife, Mary, told me she had first heard the news from her housekeeper, Margaret Talamantes, who had been watching the popular soap opera *As the World Turns*. At 12:40 P.M., Walter Cronkite interrupted the program with the unbelievable news. Mary and Merrill were in another room, packing for the trip to Austin—they were eager to hear the President speak at the gala dinner planned for that night—when Margaret came in and announced, "President Kennedy and Governor Connally have been shot!" They both rushed to the TV set, where, twenty minutes later, they heard a moist-eyed Cronkite announce in a husky voice, "President Kennedy is dead."

Of course, my main job was watching John, making sure he knew I was there, and watching over his caretakers—not that they needed any encouragement or supervision from me. I talked frequently with John's aides and kept Mary, Sheba, Adele, and Nancy Sayers, a Fort Worth friend, informed of everything that went on.

My main concern, after my husband's recovery, was the safety of our children. America's innocence had perished with John Fitzgerald Kennedy, and we now knew no one was safe, no matter how highly placed, handsome or pretty, or how charmed their life had been. For the first time in my life, I found myself in a continual state of watchful awareness: cautious and suspicious of everything. Like any mother who felt her family was threatened, my ears perked up, my eyes were sharp, and I was afraid for them for the first time.

When John moved out of intensive care, I moved with him. The hospital gave us each two additional rooms. The one next to John's contained an armed guard. Anyone seeing the patient had to walk past his station. My rooms were across the hall—a bedroom and sitting room.

Still, I was surprised after changing rooms to see a workman painting my windows black. The hospital was depressing enough without losing what little natural light we had, and I felt I had all the privacy I needed simply by pulling the shades. When I explained my desires to the staff, they only smiled. The painted windows, they said, were on instructions from the security men, who were still thick around the building. All America needed was another lunatic with a sniper's rifle, an easy target, and an insatiable urge to kill. I never complained about the hospital's decisions again.

The next day, John was fully conscious and we talked freely—but only when his tubes were removed. I held his hand and we followed events on TV, just like the rest of the world.

In Dallas, thousands of mourners placed floral wreaths and bouquets at Dealey Plaza, near the spot where the President had been slain. In the East Room of the White House, JFK lay in state on the Lincoln catafalque, a large American flag draped across his casket.

Although John's recuperation was going as well as could be expected, people were dissatisfied with reports on his condition. Now that the fate of our previous President was known and power had passed quickly to his successor—and the country was reassured that some kind of coup was not in progress—we had time to worry about other things.

Parkland's doctors and two of John's closest aides, Julian Read and George Christian, issued medical bulletins, but the press was not satisfied. The people of Texas wanted to know if their Governor was going to live or die, to be there for them in this hour of tragedy or become a victim himself.

Because of this I was asked to make a statement on television. I did not consider myself a public speaker even in the best of times, and this was undoubtedly the worst. I also knew that I was a front-row witness to what was likely the crime of the century, and that a host of lawyers, judges, and historians—as well as my fellow Texans—would judge anything and everything I had to say.

Consequently, I refused to make any public statements until I had been questioned by proper authorities.

However, the pressure continued, and I finally agreed to do it provided my statement dealt only with the Governor's condition and that I answered no questions from the press. The powers that be—in the government, the hospital, and press—agreed, and I went to work.

One of my biggest concerns was for Mrs. J. D. Tippit, wife of the Dallas police officer who had been killed early that Friday afternoon. Tippit had responded to an all points bulletin describing a suspicious man who had fled the Texas School Book Depository shortly after the shooting. The man was on foot, wearing a light, tan jacket. Two miles away, Tippit stepped from his patrol car to question a man who fit this description. The suspect was Lee Harvey Oswald.

In less time than it takes to tell, Oswald pulled a handgun and fired three shots. Officer Tippit was likely dead before his body hit the pavement.

A few minutes later, Oswald ducked inside the Texas Theater, six blocks away. An alert shoe salesmen working up the street notified police, who surrounded the building and swarmed inside. Oswald jumped from his seat, pulled his gun, and tried to fire—but the weapon jammed. Police say he was bug-eyed with rage as they wrestled him to the floor.

"I didn't kill anybody!" Oswald cried out, although nobody had accused him of anything.

The officers dragged him outside, bruised and bleeding from the tussle. The movie playing on the screen was titled *War Is Hell.*

I wanted to acknowledge Mrs. Tippitt's loss in my statement—just as Jackie had lost her husband and I had nearly lost mine—without wandering into the swamp of conspiracy theories, or pronouncing any person guilty of so heinous a crime without due process of law. Still, I had to say something, and I had to do it soon.

When it came time to read my statement, my hands were shaking so much that I could hardly hold the paper, let alone read it clearly. I was standing by a table, so I put the paper down and took my time putting on my glasses. It was the pause I needed to get myself together. I said:

The Governor is now apparently out of danger. He asked me to tell everyone he is going to be all right. John had a very, very close call. We thank God he was spared.

The Governor is in good spirits and we are deeply appreciative of the care he has received at Parkland Hospital from the doctors, the nurses, and the staff.

Governor Connally has asked me to convey to the people of Texas, the nation, and the world, our deep sorrow over the tragedy which struck at one of President Kennedy's most triumphant hours. Words cannot fully express to Mrs. Kennedy and to the President's family our feelings, which we know all Texans share.

Our son John will be our personal representative at the funeral of the President in Washington on Monday. The Governor joins me in asking that all Texans observe the day of mourning in memory of the President.

I ask that well-wishers send a donation to the family of Officer J. D. Tippit, who was shot to death trying to arrest Lee Harvey Oswald, rather than continue sending flowers and gifts to the hospital.

I then looked up from my statement and added:

We had been with the President and Mrs. Kennedy during the tour. It had been a wonderful tour and when we arrived in Dallas, and we were in the motorcade, the people could not have been friendlier, the crowd more wonderful or

more generous in their reaction to the President. The City of
Dallas does not deserve to be blamed for this ghastly crime.

I ignored the reporters shouting out their questions and went straight back to the recovery room, making sure my husband was all right, then returned to my little cell.

The Dallas police moved ahead with the case against Lee Harvey Oswald. While my husband was in intensive care, Oswald was formally arraigned and moved from the fourth floor of the Dallas jail to a cell on the third, where the Homicide Bureau could interrogate him. Gradually, John and I—and the world—learned more about this strange, troubled, and dangerous little man.

Apparently, he had been a chronic truant in school. A psychiatrist reported that he was a "potentially dangerous schizophrenic," but that didn't stop him from dropping out of high school and joining the marines. After three years in the service he had earned a marksman's medal, but had also been court-martialed twice and, eventually, received a dishonorable discharge, signed by President Kennedy's Secretary of the Navy, John B. Connally. He traveled to Moscow and, in 1959, tried to renounce his American citizenship.

But the Russians didn't want him, so in 1962—broke and depressed and full of anger—he returned to the U.S., subsidized by a loan from a federal relief agency.

While the secrets about Oswald were uncovered, Lyndon Johnson spent his first day in the Oval Office, meeting with former presidents Eisenhower and Truman and members of the Kennedy cabinet. John and I were pleased to see how well our fellow Texan was rising to the occasion. Everyone in the country needed to know that the Constitution and the government was secure, and that the orderly transition of power—even in times of unimaginable grief and loss—would continue in its uniquely American fashion.

And so it did. ✶

Chapter 7

TEXAS HOSPITALITY

*B*efore the Kennedy visit, John had been in office less than a year. No Texas governor had ever hosted a sitting President, and we were determined to do things right.

The governor's mansion in Austin, where Jack and Jackie would spend their last night, was largely unchanged from the days of Sam Houston. We had no time to perform the major renovations the place demanded, but we could certainly perk it up—make it more pleasant for our famous guests and more presentable to the nation who, through television, would be peeking over their shoulders.

I had the carpets cleaned, inspected them, then cleaned them again. I rearranged an upstairs bathroom so that Jackie would have a comfortable place to relax and powder her nose. I moved through all the rooms and hallways looking for ways to give the quaint but faintly deteriorating building a minor face-lift—to add touches of feminine warmth to its virile historical facade.

One untapped resource was the fireplace that adorned each room. As far as I knew, most of them hadn't been used since the coming of electricity, so I suggested to the caretakers that we could at least greet the Kennedys with a fire in every hearth.

"Oh, no, Mrs. Connally," one of them replied, "we can't do that. We might burn down the mansion!"

A quick inspection proved that, indeed, none of the fireplaces worked. So not only did we have no hearty fires to welcome the President, we didn't have them over Christmas or anytime during our first winter in the building. The experience did give me a new perspective, however, on Jackie's commitment to refurbish the White House. She acted not from vanity or anything like that, but because, once you live in a historic old home, you come to feel a deep sense of stewardship for the past, and a responsibility to pass that heritage forward.

A more immediate problem was the guest rooms: They simply weren't suitable for anything. The plaster was cracked on the walls and ceilings, and when anyone walked upstairs, the chandeliers below tinkled and swayed.

John was even more enthusiastic about hosting the Kennedys.

"Nellie," he said, "if the people of Texas can just get a look at him, up close, I know they will vote for him."

Politics was for John, as it was for Jack Kennedy and Lyndon Johnson, always a personal business. Nothing beats the power of a firm handshake and sparkling smile. People remember it, remember you, and take that memory to the polls. John felt a real affinity for the Kennedys, who were our age and shared John's energy and sense of vision. He knew the new President was capable of great things, as he himself had big plans for Texas. Together, he knew, their shared visions had to come true. The world did not owe us; we owed the world. And we were ready to charge.

The dates of the Texas visit had been chosen so that Jack and Jackie could return to Washington in time for their children's birthdays—John-John would be three years old on Monday, and Caroline would turn six a few days later.

By a cruel twist of fate, that Monday would be the date of their father's funeral.

As the date of the visit drew closer, we grew more

confident in our ability to host the President and First Lady—and through the media, the country and the world—but one problem remained.

Kennedy would be welcomed in Texas, but Dallas had had a couple of political incidents when it came to liberal politicians. The conservative fringe turned out in droves to taunt ranking democrats—even Lyndon Johnson had been spat upon—and someone once struck Adlai Stevenson on the head with a homemade sign. It was a place where a cordial visit could turn ugly, and that cold shoulder wouldn't help anyone. John wasn't concerned about violence—nobody in those days was—just an embarrassing situation played out on national television.

The White House put out the story that Kennedy's real mission in Texas was to resolve a long and bitter feud between Vice President Johnson and Ralph Yarborough, the state's ranking senator and leader of the liberal wing of the Democratic Party. That, of course, was nonsense. If Kennedy wanted to mend political fences, he could do so easily, and perhaps more effectively, from Washington, where Johnson and Yarborough worked and lived.

The truth is, President Kennedy had been pressing Johnson for months to visit Texas and was eager to raise money for the 1964 campaign. Back in June 1963, John and his administrative assistant Larry Temple were with the two of them in El Paso, where Kennedy pleaded with the Vice President and John to host a fundraising tour.

John had resisted the trip because he was uncomfortable about trying to raise a lot of money in the state after such a close election. Kennedy was not all that popular at the time with many traditional contributors in Texas.

To understand the political picture of the day, it is important to remember that despite the fact that Dwight Eisenhower carried Texas for the Republicans in 1952 and 1956, Texas in the early sixties was a heavily Democratic state. But the party was sharply divided between liberal Democrats, personified by Senator Yarborough, and conservative Democrats—most of the state's power structure that supported John Connally. The Vice President had support from both factions, but was often opposed by Yarborough and the liberals.

The White House persisted in its zeal for a presidential visit. The original plan called for multiple fundraiser events in major Texas cities. That was when John—ever the political pragmatist—stepped in with a dose of common sense.

Too many fundraisers would make it look like Kennedy was squeezing the state—not a good image with the election that was less than a year away.

Instead, John wanted the President to meet Texans of all political persuasions in a less political environment. Although polls at the time showed the Governor running well ahead of the President in Texas, John was confident Kennedy could carry the state again if people got to know him better.

So the plan was modified. With John using his influence with the state's leadership, along with the Vice President's supporters, a series of nonpartisan events was planned.

The one purely political event was to be a Friday-night fundraising dinner in Austin, the climax of the visit. Tickets were priced at $100 each—a princely sum in those days. Even that one political fundraiser was not greeted with initial success. Although Kennedy was well liked by Texas liberals, conservatives were more lukewarm. Originally, Democratic Party officials and the White House were supposed to spearhead ticket sales. But when those effects were flagging, John stepped in and took to the telephone to motivate his own legion of supporters to buy tickets. By Friday, the Austin fundraiser was sure to be a big success.

Under the revised plan, John and I would join the President in San Antonio Thursday morning, along with the Vice President and Mrs. Johnson. That afternoon, the President would dedicate a new research facility for the School of Aerospace Medicine at Brooke Army Medical Center, then attend a testimonial dinner in Houston for Albert Thomas, the congressman who, along with Lyndon Johnson, had been most instrumental in bringing Kennedy's ambitious space program to Texas.

Friday would be our busiest day. It would begin with an early outdoor rally and civic breakfast in Fort Worth, followed by a luncheon in Dallas and a gala dinner in Austin

In honor of
President John F. Kennedy
and
Vice President Lyndon B. Johnson

The State Democratic Executive Committee
requests the pleasure of your company
at the
Texas Welcome Dinner
on Friday evening the twenty-second of November
One thousand nine hundred and sixty-three
at half after seven o'clock
at the Municipal Auditorium
in the City of Austin

Contribution card enclosed
Optional dress

Mr. Eugene M. Locke, Chairman
Mrs. Alfred Negley, Vice-Chairman
Mr. Frank C. Erwin, Jr., Secretary

President, United States of America

Vice President, United States of America

Governor, State of Texas

TEXAS WELCOME DINNER

NOVEMBER 22, 1963, MUNICIPAL AUDITORIUM, AUSTIN, TEXAS

PROGRAM

Eugene M. Locke, Master of Ceremonies, Chairman, State Democratic Executive Committee

Music by Volunteers from The University of Texas Longhorn Band. Vincent R. DiNino, Director.

Entrance of National and State Official Guests at Head Tables

Invocation by Dr. Robert Tate, Minister of the First Methodist Church of Austin

The National Anthem

Introduction of Members of the State Democratic Executive Committee by Eugene M. Locke

Introduction of Members of the Texas House of Representatives by Speaker Byron Tunnell

Introduction of Members of the Texas Senate by Lieutenant Governor Preston Smith

Introduction of Guests at Head Tables by Eugene M. Locke

Entrance of Governor and Mrs. John Connally

Entrance of Vice President and Mrs. Lyndon B. Johnson

Entrance of President and Mrs. John F. Kennedy

Welcome by Governor Connally

Remarks by Vice President Johnson

Address by President Kennedy

Benediction by the Very Reverend Edward C. Matocha, Chancellor of the Diocese of Texas

LYNDON B. JOHNSON

JOHN F. KENNEDY

JOHN CONNALLY

following two receptions for the state legislature at the governor's mansion—the most overtly political event on the crowded schedule, and a concession to the White House John was happy to make.

"They'll be charmed by him," John predicted, referring to the legislators. "They'll go back to their districts and tell everybody that they spoke with the President. They're going to be his goodwill ambassadors."

The other big concession John made was the motorcade in Dallas. The President's advance team insisted that we have one, but John and his staff were opposed. Aside from the risks of an embarrassing confrontation with street demonstrators, John wanted Jack rested and ready, not exhausted, when he met the entire Texas legislature that evening.

But politics, both men knew, is a personal business. Nothing beats seeing the candidate in the flesh, even if it's through the bubble roof of a fast-moving car. In the end, the White House got its way.

Three days before the visit, newspapers published the route of the motorcade. That wasn't part of the agreement, and John was livid. He didn't want the President's movements publicized.

He was afraid there would be hecklers. ✳

Chapter 8

A BEAUTIFUL DAY
IN DALLAS

✦

I left Austin for San Antonio at noon on Thursday, November 21. John was in Houston and would arrive shortly after me. It had been almost two years since I had seen the Kennedys, and although John and Jack had been in touch for various reasons, a lot had changed in the meantime. I was looking forward to renewing our friendship.

My plane touched down and taxied to the terminal, where I received a red carpet welcome. It was a nice and unexpected honor for a Texas First Lady, but I suspect it was left over

from the official welcome for LBJ and Lady Bird, who'd arrived earlier and greeted me in the building.

John arrived next, and shortly thereafter, air traffic around the airport was cleared and Air Force One came into view. The magnificent silver, red, and white jet touched down gently and taxied to what had now become the "official" red carpet.

The four of us went out to welcome the Kennedys, and although crowds and reporters were nothing new to me, I felt especially nervous. In those days, political wives were judged first on their appearance, second by their demeanor, and third for what—if anything—they had to say. My biggest concern was that my outfit, which complemented Lady Bird's, wouldn't clash with Jackie's. I hoped they would like their gifts: watercolors by famed San Antonio artist Julian Onderdonk,

given to me by Nancy Negley to present to the First Couple. Certainly, within the next twenty-four hours, my concerns and priorities would change drastically, to say the least.

The big plane's door opened and Jackie stepped onto the stairs. After the usual collective sigh that accompanied her appearance, the crowd applauded and Jackie waved. She wore a white dress with black accessories—very East Coast. She would look very stylish and sophisticated.

Right behind her came her husband, Jack Kennedy, tanned and smiling. He smoothed his tie, tucking the tip under his buttoned jacket, pushed a shock of hair away from his forehead, and the crowd went wild.

After a brief ceremony at the base of the stairs, we all got into the Lincoln and started our motorcade to Brooke Medical

Center for the President's first speech. The crowd lining the road was large and friendly, chanting *Jack! Jackie! Jack! Jackie!* as we passed. The President and First Lady smiled, waved back, and couldn't have looked more pleased.

At Brooke we got out, worked our way into the building, then back out onto a platform facing a large crowd. I sat between Lyndon Johnson and Eugene Zuckert, Secretary of the Air Force. He introduced President Kennedy, who then made a fine speech—apparently, the only kind he knew how to deliver. The crowd, composed mostly of Air Force and facility personnel and their families, responded warmly.

While the Kennedys moved on to inspect a second building, John and I returned to the President's car, which wheeled around the building to pick them up on the other side. A Secret Service car followed us—standard procedure when the President is traveling—and the Johnsons' car followed that.

After picking them up, we returned to the airport, where John and I boarded Air Force One for the short hop to Houston and the dinner honoring Texas Congressman Albert Thomas. Even in those days, the President and Vice President usually traveled in separate planes. Although it was an era before assassins and terrorists would make their mark on American politics, mechanical failure, bad weather, and pilot error could always turn a routine flight into a tragedy.

John and I spent the short flight in a small sitting room next to the presidential bedroom. Jackie sat with us for a few

minutes, then retired to get some rest. I always got the sense that "being on"—the stock-in-trade for politicians and their wives—was a lot of work for her and tired her out. That's another reason, I think, she got the reputation of being a little cool and aloof, which—given her strong character and deep feelings for Jack and her children—was mostly undeserved.

Not so with Jack Kennedy. He was a politician's politician, loved to talk, and loved even more to listen. That was one of his great strengths. Even when his back was killing him, he'd participate in, if not preside over, any discussion with enthusiasm. Today he chatted amiably with us, Albert Thomas (plus several congressmen accompanying him), and Senator Ralph Yarborough—though Yarborough eventually left to ride with the staff at the front of the plane. Since John was a Lyndon Johnson "crony," the two didn't get along. So much for the President mending fences on this trip.

After landing in Houston, we went straight to the hotel and dressed for dinner. On the way to the banquet, we stopped briefly at a LULAC meeting, where the President made some remarks. The Thomas testimonial went well, and the Kennedys looked marvelous. Jackie wore a black suit.

After the dinner we returned to the airport and boarded Air Force One. Our next stop was Carswell Air Force Base in Fort Worth, where we arrived after eleven P.M. Although it was pitch black everywhere but near the buildings, a large crowd lined the road from the base to our hotel, where we found an even bigger mob in the street and in the lobby.

Everyone was exhausted, so we all went directly to our suites. I went to bed, but since it was so late and our start the next day was so early, John and some staffers went downstairs for breakfast—hot coffee and eggs—before turning in. After all, Fort Worth had been our home at one point, and he wanted to see his old friends. He was in his element—playing host to the most powerful man in the world, orchestrating events on a grand scale—having earned every speck of the honor, trust, and responsibility bestowed on him through his own hard work and dedication. I couldn't have loved him more.

Friday, November 22, dawned under gray and soggy clouds. The parking lot across from the Texas Hotel, where the President was to make his first appearance of the day,

was slick with rain. A few people with umbrellas had already gathered in front of the wet platform, and more trickled in each minute, but it was an unsettling start to our most ambitious day.

I started to dress in a white suit, complemented with black accessories. I was glad I hadn't worn it the previous day, as originally planned, or Jackie and I would've looked like twins—and believe me, you didn't want to get involved in a fashion contest with Jackie.

But the weather was so bad and wintry, I decided to wear a much warmer two-piece pink wool suit. John, lucky creatures that men are, was dressed and gone for his first appearance with the President downstairs.

Eventually, a staffer came and escorted me to a salon near the hotel's grand dining room, where a huge breakfast— hosting almost three thousand people—was about to begin. John was speaking privately with Jack, then the President turned and spoke to Senator Yarborough.

Arriving at a formal function, even a huge, impersonal breakfast, is always a ritual affair. Those of us at the head table were assembled and led in, in reverse order of rank. After we wives and senior staffers were seated, John, the Vice President, and their contingent of congressmen marched in, followed immediately by the President and the remaining representatives. Jackie wasn't with either party, though a place for her at our table was left open.

The organizer made introductions, and I was beginning to worry that something had gone wrong. Where was Jackie? Was she sick? Distracted by a call about her children? Anything seemed possible in that surreal environment. President Kennedy remarked, "Nobody asks what Lyndon and I are wearing. It takes Jackie longer, but she looks better than we do when she arrives."

Then, exactly on cue, the First Lady made her entrance. She wore a beautiful pink wool suit—I had chosen wrong. I shouldn't have worried. People burst spontaneously into applause, stood up, and crowded into the aisles to get a better view. We all rose, even the President, when she reached the table, and Jack greeted her affectionately. If anything personified the Kennedy magic—what they meant to America and the world—it was embodied in that moment.

Jack Kennedy made a great speech that morning, after the rain-soaked rally in the parking lot across the street. Minutes were precious, but it had been arranged for the President to call John Nance "Cactus Jack" Garner, the first Vice President ever elected from Texas, at his home in Uvalde to wish him a happy 95th birthday. He had been born on November 22, 1868. Then we piled into the now-familiar limos for the return trip to the Carswell air base. This time, I rode with the Johnsons—I was happy to have some time to visit with Lady Bird—and an unusual fourth passenger. Kennedy, it seems, was a little miffed that Senator

Yarborough had snubbed him on Air Force One—preferring to ride in front with the staff instead of in the presidential lounge. He had already insulted the Vice President once by refusing to ride with him from the air base, and again that morning in the salon with their skirmish before breakfast. Now the President himself informed Senator Yarborough that he would ride with the Johnsons, or walk!

I may have been assigned to the Johnson car as peacekeeper—I really don't know. But when I found out about the arrangements, I chose to ride in front with the Secret Service men. And I did.

The crowds lining the road to the airport were wet but cheerful. There is probably some formula for calculating devotion by a citizen's willingness to come out on a cold, wet day to cheer a politician. If so, the Kennedys' score must have been pretty high. I started running through the day's upcoming events in my head, making sure I hadn't forgotten any important details.

After our flight to Dallas, we would attend a luncheon at the Trade Mart, then return to Austin for the legislative reception and gala banquet. I was confident that we had done everything we could to get the governor's mansion into shape for a presidential visit, even planning what our three children would wear. Their photograph with the President and First Lady, I knew, would become an heirloom passed down to their own children and grandchildren, and I wanted both the memory and the keepsake to be perfect. Little did I know that their treasured picture would never be taken.

The plane ride was uneventful, and bad tempers, if any remained, seemed to cool. We landed at Love Field and taxied to the tarmac, where a friendly crowd was waiting. John was visibly relieved at the lack of demonstrations or hostile signs of any kind. When the plane's door opened and the Kennedys stepped out, even the clouds themselves miraculously parted and drenched the scene in sunlight.

We were sure the rest of the day would go as well. ✳

Chapter 9

THE SPLIT SCREEN

O n Sunday after the assassination, church bells tolled across the nation. Millions prayed for the Kennedys, for our new President, and for the country.

In Dallas, morning services at six hundred churches drew record crowds. In American cities everywhere, citizens watched on TV the solemn procession of Kennedy's cortege from the White House to the rotunda of the Capitol. As in Lincoln's funeral procession in April 1865 almost a hundred years before, "the silence," one newspaper reported, "was profound" despite the enormous crowd.

I was standing by John's bed when the TV picture switched to the underground garage of the Dallas police station. An armored car waited to transfer Lee Harvey Oswald from the city to the county jail. The now-familiar face with its dazed, combative look, high forehead, and mussed hair appeared flanked by two officers, with Dallas police captain Will Fritz, in a western hat, leading the way. Then, in stunned disbelief, we watched a strange man in a business suit jump in front of Oswald and fire a single shot.

The deputies reacted quickly and wrestled the gunman to the ground, but it was another of those strange moments in a week filled with unearthly images. We just couldn't believe our eyes.

Numbly, I asked, "John—what happened? What was that?"

He answered, "Nellie, that man just shot Oswald."

Half an hour later, we heard a commotion in the hall outside John's room. I looked out and a convoy of police, nurses, and attendants were wheeling the accused assassin by on a hospital gurney—headed for the same operating room where a scant two days earlier they had saved my husband's life.

I wish I could have been more charitable, or at least appreciated the irony of the situation, but all I felt was uncontrollable rage. Here was the man who probably killed our President and tried to kill my husband, and who had certainly killed Officer Tippit, being treated to the finest emergency care our city had to offer. One of the doctors, in fact, was none other than Malcolm Perry, the same physician who, that previous Friday, had tried to hard to revive President Kennedy. I simply couldn't believe it!

We learned shortly thereafter that Jack Ruby had shot Oswald point-blank in the stomach with a .38 revolver. His spleen, pancreas, liver, and one kidney had been pulverized. Though his vital signs were slipping even as they placed him on the table, the surgeons tried hard to save his life. After all, that was their job.

When I heard that Oswald was dead, I didn't feel any sadness or sympathy. Sorry he was dead? No. But I knew that from the standpoint of history, of truth and clarity, his death was going to have unending repercussions. He died before anyone could obtain any admission, any information, from him.

The man who killed the killer turned out to be the owner of a tawdry Dallas strip joint called the Colony Club. He was well known to the police as a kind of redneck, law-enforcement groupie, which may have explained how he was able to get so close, unchallenged, to his victim. When they finally got him under control and disarmed him, his only cry was "Hey—you know me! I'm Jack Ruby!" as if they should treat him like a hero.

From **LOVE FIELD**

After that strangest of days, with the screen split three ways, we were afraid to watch television but were afraid if we didn't. The world had swung out of orbit. Our screen was certainly divided into so many parts. ✦

Chapter 10

BURYING A PRESIDENT

✦

*I*n the midst of all this confusion, the White House asked if I would attend the funeral of President Kennedy on Monday.

It was impossible for me to leave my husband a mere three days after he was almost killed, so instead I suggested sending our oldest son, John III, who had already shown he was capable of thinking quickly and had his dad's noble heart. The Johnsons graciously accepted our compromise and included him in their official party.

Now, John III, as you may have guessed, was and is a serious, high-minded fellow. Several people who met him at the funeral thought at first he was a Secret Service agent—he was that mature and self-possessed.

Before leaving Dallas, John III came to my little room and held out a pad of paper and fountain pen. He said, "I want you to write a letter to Mrs. Kennedy for me to take to the funeral."

I replied, "I don't think I can. What could I possibly say?

The President is dead. Your father is going to live—" At least we were almost sure. "I don't think I can find any words."

John III stood over me. He said nothing, just held out the paper and pen. It was the most eloquent exhortation I had yet heard to overcome my fears and inhibitions. I took the pen and wrote quickly:

Dear Jackie,

With all my heart, I long to be with you today. John's condition is still too serious for me to leave.

We just want you to know how very much we care as we share your grief and join you in prayer.

John and I send you our love.

Nellie Connally
Saturday, November 23, 1963

My husband and I watched the funeral on the small black-and-white TV in his room at Parkland Memorial. By this time the workmen had not only painted my windows black but had installed a two-inch-thick steel plate over the glass in John's bedroom. Guards were on duty around the clock.

We watched the procession move down Pennsylvania

Avenue: the caisson with the magnificent, riderless horse and the two boots turned backward in the stirrups, heading toward Arlington Cemetery. So many painful images came flooding back at that moment. It was all so hard to believe, so agonizing to watch.

We squinted at the little screen, trying hard to spot our son in the crowd. He was standing with Presidents Eisenhower and Truman at the funeral, and he left with the Johnson family, but we did not see him. Our hearts swelled with pride and we marveled again at how much the world can change in a mere four days. The country had been turned upside down, inside out. Our young son had become a man.

After the services, John III told us later, he walked down the hill with President and Mrs. Johnson to a limousine where Jackie and Robert Kennedy were waiting. Jackie and Bobby quickly stepped out to greet the new President.

Lyndon Johnson introduced our son to the Kennedys—the meeting that was supposed to have taken place under vastly different circumstances the previous Friday at the Austin gala. John said to Mrs. Kennedy, "I would like to express the personal sorrow of my family and of the people of the State of Texas at your terrible loss."

Jackie took our son's hand in both of hers and said, "John, tell your mother that I am so glad your father is going to be all right. That's the only good thing that has come of this."

John said his overwhelming impression was that he had just met the most gracious lady. That was Jackie. That was our son.

A few days after the funeral, I received a letter from the former First Lady. It was dated December 1, 1963, and I still have it. It was written in her hand on elegant blue stationery.

I have chosen not to reproduce this personal letter in its entirety, out of consideration for Jackie and her family.

She wrote to say that she had seen our son at the funeral. What she said about my husband moved me greatly, and she confided comforting words about our shared ordeal. She wrote that the four of us were very much the same, and the two of us, women who truly loved their husbands: "We loved them every way that a woman can love a man, haven't we, and so fortunate to have them in our arms at that terrible time." I felt the same way.

She asked me to tell John that she was so glad he was alive. She said, "Please tell him not to forget Jack. I know he won't."

I have not forgotten either of you for forty years and I never will for however many years I have left. ✶

Chapter 11

JOHN, SHARON, AND MARK

$\mathcal{M}$any years after those terrible events, at my request for this book, my three children put their recollections on paper. First, Sharon (now Mrs. Robert Amman):

I just had my fourteenth birthday on November 17, and was in O. Henry High School (named after the fabled author, who lived in Austin). It was just like any other day at school, but I was excited about the upcoming visit from the President and First

Lady. Mom had bought me a new dress for this important event.

It was my lunch hour and as usual my friends and I had all gathered to head for the cafeteria. The rule of the school was NO RUNNING, so we walked briskly to get a good table. As we all sat down, the principal and some counselors came in and seemed to be looking at me. I quickly turned and asked my friends if I had been running. They said no.

Just then the adults all walked over to me and the cafeteria grew so quiet when the principal said, "Sharon, I would like to see you in my office." My heart started beating so fast and my mind was racing to think of what I had done. When we walked out I could hear everybody whispering, "Poor Sharon, what did she do?"

When we got to the principal's office, he shut the door. He and a female counselor both looked at me with tears in their eyes. I was so scared. He said, "Sharon, President Kennedy and your daddy have been shot." I just looked at them for a moment and I thought I was going to throw up. Shot meant DEAD to me. I started crying and they tried to comfort me and told me that they weren't sure of my dad's condition. They said the mansion guards were on the way, with my two brothers, to pick me up.

By then a friend, Libby Drake, was outside the office and they told me that Libby would walk me to my locker to get my coat. I was so weak and so scared, it seemed very unreal to me. I had the locker door open and was reaching in to get my coat and purse, when a boy ran around the corner so quickly that he slipped and started sliding toward me and Libby.

But he was screaming, "Libby, Libby, did you hear that Governor Connally and President Kennedy are both dead?' She started screaming, "Shut up, shut up!" I closed the locker door and the boy looked at me just horrified at what he had said, not knowing that it was me with my head in the locker. I just sat down and started sobbing.

Libby was trying to console me by telling me that this

guy was an idiot and he didn't know anything. I so wanted to believe her, but I was frightened. She helped me gather my things and walked me to the front door of the school, where the guards had now arrived and my big brother, Johnny, was with them.

I was so happy to see him and we just hugged and he held my hand and walked me to the car. We didn't say anything until we got inside and my little brother, Mark, was sitting in the car, waiting for us. Johnny assured us that the boy was wrong and that Daddy was going to be okay. I didn't know if he knew that for sure, but I wanted to believe him, so I did.

The car raced back to the mansion, where there was much security and confusion. I remember Linda Bird Johnson being there, and members of Dad's staff, but it was all kind of a blur. We were all just anxiously awaiting a call from Mama. We knew she would let us hear from her as soon as she could. Finally, the call came and she told us that Daddy had been shot pretty badly, but he was going to recover. We wanted to talk to Dad, but Mom said not just yet. She said she would call soon and give us an update.

I don't remember exactly when, but my grandmother (Katie Brill, my mom's mom) came and I felt better having her with us. Everyone was being so wonderful to us, but having our grandmother (family) was very comforting. Katie was a very warm and wonderful lady and very strong. We prayed for Daddy and the President.

Mark, a little boy with big eyes, saw the events from a different perspective:

I recall being in my sixth-grade class, waiting for the day to end, because later that evening I was going to meet the President and Mrs. Kennedy. I was surprised to see my brother, John, arrive early to pick me up. He was with a DPS officer from the governor's mansion and seemed to be in a hurry.

We hustled out of the classroom and, once in the car, raced out of the parking lot. We hit speeds of up to eighty miles an hour. I thought we must really be late for something. I do not recall asking for, or getting, any explanations. Shortly, we arrived at my sister's school. It was clear that something was wrong when the DPS officer and another man (her principal) walked Sharon to the car, one on each arm, almost holding her up. She was limp and crying and visibly upset.

At this point, John had to tell me that there had been a shooting in Dallas and that Dad and the President both had been shot. He did not know how they were doing and we had not gotten an official report. I just kind of went numb.

I will never forget the scene at the mansion. As an eleven-year old, I had rarely seen grown people cry. Maybe one or two at a funeral. By the time we arrived, a fairly large number of people were on hand. Most of them were openly weeping. This scene really elevated my sense of fear and anxiety. John was trying to reach the hospital in Dallas and the operator was unable to get through. She knew she had the family on the line and she was crying too.

After an hour of trying, John did get through. Despite instructions otherwise, he told Sharon and me that he was flying to Dallas. We wanted to go with him, or have him stay. As it turned out, he went on and we stayed with our grandparents.

I remember being scared, feeling lost and overwhelmed. I did not know how to react to the situation or all the attention.

We finally did get a believable report that Dad was alive and going into surgery. We actually heard this announcement on television. The surgery lasted five hours. Finally, I wore out emotionally. I went to my room and climbed into bed. Whether out of exhaustion or just as a place to escape the moment, this seemed like a safe place to be. I slept through most of the surgery.

I was awakened to hear the report from the doctors when they said Dad had survived the operation and was going to live. We were so excited; Sharon and I wanted to be there with Mother and our big brother. But it wasn't until several days later that we were able to join them in Dallas.

I had never seen my dad in anything but perfect health and a picture of strength, but the sight of him in the hospital was quite different. It was clear he had been through a very tough time. His arm was in a cast and his fingers were wired in place. It was really very frightening.

He had Thanksgiving dinner with us, but he was still weak and did not stay with us for very long. After we left, the nurses turned off the Texas versus Texas A&M football game. Texas was behind and Dad was upset because he wanted to see Texas make a great, late comeback to win the game. But they were concerned for his condition.

Throughout the whole experience, I had the benefit of being able to lean on Sharon or John, who had to be strong for all of us. Aside from Mother, it must have been the most difficult for John.

Sometime later, while Dad was still in his cast and sling, President Johnson came to the governor's mansion. I ran up and threw my arms around him and greeted him as "Uncle Lyndon."

Respectfully, Dad told me I should now call him "Mr. President."

President Johnson just smiled and said, "I'm still your Uncle Lyndon."

Our older son represented us with poise and dignity at the funeral of President Kennedy. In all these years, we had never asked him to write down what he saw or thought or felt, until now:

I flew that Sunday afternoon on a state plane to Washington, D.C. When we landed, I was taken to the Elms, which was then the official residence of the Vice President.

This was the home of Lyndon Johnson, who was now the President of the United States.

Mrs. Kennedy and her family were still living in the White House, and the new President had invited them to stay as long as they needed. I arrived at the Elms and was met by President, Mrs. Johnson, and their daughter Luci. Being with the Johnsons did not seem all that strange in one sense. Our families had been very close throughout my entire life and had even shared a duplex in Austin for a time.

On the other hand, there was a surreal quality about the Johnson household that night, as well. They were as shocked and unhappy as the rest of us and yet had been thrust immediately into the role of calming the nation and carrying on with government.

A number of President Johnson's trusted friends and advisors moved through the Elms that night. I remember seeing Jack Valenti, who had flown up on Air Force One with the Johnsons after the assassination, and Abe Fortas, a lawyer and advisor to the President. I remember spending some time that evening visiting with Mrs. Fortas, who was an attorney herself.

The Johnsons were concerned about my father, and what news I had of him and his condition, and how my mother was doing. I gave them all of the information that I could.

At some point during the evening, Luci Johnson and I went with a United States Secret Service escort to view President Kennedy's body, which was lying in state in the rotunda of the

United States Capitol. The lines stretched many people abreast from the Capitol all the way down Pennsylvania Avenue until very late in the evening. We were able to drive directly to the Capitol and were escorted through a private entrance and into the rotunda, where we were then able to pay our respects to the fallen President. We then drove directly back to the Elms.

On the morning of President Kennedy's funeral, we rose and dressed and then drove from the Elms to the private entrance to the White House. President Johnson had apparently made the decision that I was to stay with the family. I rode with them in the limousine on a jump seat in the back. Upon arriving at the White House we walked through the executive mansion and out the front door, under the covered drive on the Pennsylvania Avenue side.

As a seventeen-year-old participating in these events, I was not thinking about being with the President of the United States or walking through the White House. My thoughts were on the funeral that we were about to attend and on the bereaved family. When we walked out the front entrance of the White House I was literally a step off the right shoulder of President Johnson. As soon as we cleared the door, an unknown secret service agent grabbed me and began to pull me away. Almost instantly, the head of the President's detail grabbed the other agent and said "No, that's Governor Connally's son." I was immediately returned to the side of the President. It occurred to me at that moment that I was simply a dark-haired young man in an overcoat and that very few people knew who I was or why I was there.

As we emerged above the covered drive, the entire funeral procession was already in place in the driveway. To our right were some one hundred and fifty world leaders, including the President of France, the emperor of Ethiopia, former presidents Eisenhower and Truman, and others. To our left was the entire Kennedy family, standing and waiting.

Normally, at a funeral everyone defers to the family of the deceased. They arrive last and everyone waits on them. Since my mind and heart were focused in that direction, it was a shock to me that the Kennedy family was standing in the drive and waiting on us. They were, of course, showing the respect due to the President of the United States.

We took our place in the procession immediately behind the Kennedy family. I walked a step behind President Johnson and a step to his right, shoulder to shoulder with his military aide, who carried the appropriate codes for the day. We walked in the procession from the White House to St. Matthew's Cathedral for the funeral mass. In certain news clips, I can be seen walking behind the President. I suppose that most people thought that I was another secret service agent.

The walk in that funeral procession was an experience hard to describe. The drums were beautiful and somber, the sight of the caisson rolling forward, the riderless horse

with the boots turned backward in the stirrups, the Kennedy family walking in front of us. Huge crowds lined the route of the procession and were totally silent. It was a time of terrible sadness and loss. I had no present feelings of being a part of something historic or special or unusual for someone so young. As everyone else there, I was simply overcome by the sadness and the unreal nature of these events.

We sat in reserved seating at the funeral mass and afterward we again climbed into the presidential limousine, where I rode in the back with the family. It was originally discussed to walk the distance from St. Matthews to Arlington cemetery, but the Kennedy family decided it was too far and we therefore were riding in cars.

In the back of the Johnson limousine there was very little conversation. Everyone was too sad and the situation was too grim. The crowds were huge and the people were again very quiet and respectful. Although we were riding, we were moving at a walking pace and there were agents walking near the presidential limousine.

When we got to Arlington National Cemetery, we drove as close to the gravesite as was possible and exited the presidential limousine. We then approached the gravesite where, again, virtually all the other parties were already in place. As we approached, I separated from the Johnsons. They proceeded to reserved seating with the Kennedy family on one side of the eternal flame.

I walked into a group of other mourners on the side next to the family. The service that followed was again beautiful and sad and appropriate and once again I had little thought for the people around me or for the historical significance of that event. Only at the end of the service, as everyone began to move away from the gravesite, did I notice that I had been standing near former presidents Eisenhower and Truman.

I rejoined the Johnsons as we walked toward the cars.

On our way down the slope, the Johnsons took me with them toward the Kennedy limousine. Mrs. Kennedy was inside the car and as we approached the vehicle I imagined that they would roll the window down and we would lean in to pay our respects. I was startled when, as we approached the car, the door opened and Mrs. Kennedy and Attorney General Robert Kennedy got out of the car to greet us.

Once again, I was thinking in terms of the family of the deceased and they were, even at this difficult time, paying their respects to the office of the President of the United States. President and Mrs. Johnson shook hands with Attorney General Kennedy and Mrs. Kennedy, and expressed their condolences. They introduced me to the Attorney General, who shook my hand and nodded. His face was ashen and tear streaked and virtually without expression.

They then introduced me to Mrs. Kennedy, whose veil was still down and still glistened with her tears as well. She took my hand and I said, "I would like to express the personal

sorrow of my family and of the people of the State of Texas at your terrible loss."

Still holding onto my hand, she said, "Please tell your mother that I am so glad your father is going to be all right. That's the only good thing that has come of this."

I said, "I have brought a note from my mother." I gave it to her and she said, Thank you, and they both got back into their car.

President and Mrs. Johnson and I then walked back to the presidential limousine. We retraced our drive from Arlington and went directly back to the Elms.

It seemed to me that the whole period, from the time that I learned of the assassination until some days later, was an unearthly experience. My thoughts were focused on my father, my mother, my brother and sister, and also upon the Kennedys and the Johnsons and our state and nation.

I had no thoughts during those days of how unusual it was for a seventeen-year-old to be participating in those events. They were not happy times. They were not exciting times. They were sad and emotional times. Only in looking back over the years have I been able to place those events in their historical context.

They changed the life of our country and of my family forever. ✳

Chapter 12

TESTIMONY

*O*f all the changes that bombarded us in the weeks that followed, the worst was destroying the innocent routines of my children.

Before the assassination, I had tried to let them live as normal a life as possible. Mark loved to walk along the low wall that surrounded the governor's mansion, but those days were gone forever. Sharon loved visit with her girlfriends, but she could no longer leave the grounds without an escort. That, perhaps, was the worst part of it all. By the act of one lunatic,

our world had been changed forever. Something priceless had been lost: our sense of security, our personal freedom. It would be a long, long time before I stopped feeling compelled to look over my shoulder. Eternal vigilance, they say, is the price of liberty. Now it had become our way of life.

Five days after the shots rang out, it was Thanksgiving. Ironically, in this worst of all years, we had a lot to be thankful about.

The hospital orderlies moved a large table and some extra chairs into the guard's room. They put a white tablecloth over the Formica top and set out some flatware from the cafeteria. A moment later, my children and I were presented with a roast turkey and all the trimmings, compliments of the hospital kitchen. Best of all, John joined us at the table. The doctors were skeptical of this plan, but John insisted. They brought him in, trussed up like a turkey himself, with all his tubes and pulleys and surgical retaining wires. Sharon and Mark were shaken by his pale, emaciated appearance, but were ecstatic just to be near him. In the worst of times, it was the best Thanksgiving ever.

Out of these horrors, we received many gifts. The best were completely spiritual. I once said to my sister-in-law, Mary Connally, "God took John too soon. He had so much more to give."

She replied, "Nellie, He gave you thirty years! What more do you want?"

"Well," I said, "I just want twenty more!"

During the long weeks of John's recovery—in the hospital and back home—we both suffered from what people today would call posttraumatic stress.

Although I learned to sleep comfortably after a time, my waking life was a constant battle against intruding images of that day: the terrible noise, the President's startled eyes, John's crumpled body and blood-soaked shirt, Jackie's hollow-eyed stare across the hall.

Our first night together, John cried out in his sleep. I tried to comfort him, and asked him the next morning what had happened—a nightmare? Pain from his wounds?

He said that in his dreams, people were always shooting at him, chasing him. I asked who these people were and he couldn't answer. Just different people in different places, but always with guns. He didn't like talking about it and I didn't like asking—I had been there myself in my dreams and was not eager to return to that hellish world; so over the next few weeks, whenever he cried out, I simply patted him gently on the shoulder and said nothing. Eventually, the demons faded for both of us, but we knew we'd have to live with them, in one form or another, for the rest of our lives.

Ten days after the President was killed and my husband was shot, and just two days after he came home—twenty pounds lighter, right arm in a cast and sling, I went off to a quiet place in the mansion with pens, pencils, and yellow pads, and wrote—what happened in that car.

I did not write it for history or for you—just for my grandchildren and all the little Connallys to come in case they had an interest (after reading in their school history books that their great-great-grandparents were in that car) in what happened on that terrible day when President John F. Kennedy was assassinated, and their grandfather almost killed. A horrible time in Texas and U.S. history.

I did not go back and add to it after so much else became known later. I just put it in the bottom drawer of an old file cabinet and let it gather dust for thirty-three years.

When we finally got John home and settled in, I treated myself to a trip to the beauty shop. In those days, that's what ladies did when they felt worn down and worn out: They got their hair done. My hairdresser in Austin put me in the chair, looked me over like a Parkland surgeon, then gave a low whistle.

"Mrs. Connally," he said. "Did you know there is a streak of white hair, two inches wide, down the back of your head?"

I sat bolt upright and reached for the mirror. "No, I didn't! It wasn't there three weeks ago!"

Shortly thereafter I made an appointment with our family doctor. During the routine physical, I asked him what might have caused the white streak.

"Shock," he said matter-of-factly. "From what you say, you never screamed or even cried until after the event. You kept everything inside. That's what happens to good little soldiers."

That was the first time it really dawned on me what toll that terrible time had taken. Just because you escape the bullets doesn't mean you escape the scars.

In January, we flew to Washington to testify before the Warren Commission. John could walk, but his arm was still in a sling.

Our hotel room was filled literally wall-to-wall with flowers. I chose an especially beautiful arrangement of yellow roses and took them to Arlington Cemetery the

next day, so John and I could place them by the Eternal Flame at Jack's grave site. Afterward, we stood silently for several minutes, unable, somehow, to pull ourselves away. We made the pilgrimage alone. The next day, a picture of us standing solemnly by the flame appeared in the newspapers, so a reporter must have followed us or, perhaps, snapped his picture from a distance through a telephoto lens.

We phoned Jackie's residence on that trip, worrying less about seeing her than simply letting her know we were there and that we cared. She was sleeping when we called, and from my own experience, I was glad to hear it. Our pain, both physical and emotional, had been terrible. Hers must've been beyond all human endurance.

Testifying before the Warren Commission was, to say the least, another otherworldly experience. Our concern about evidence and history started well before we were called to Washington.

In November, I had spent the longest day of my life in the blood-soaked pink suit I'd put on that fatal morning in Fort Worth. My friend Nancy Sayers (now Abington) took it to be cleaned, though I vowed I'd never look at it—let alone wear it—again. Still, it was "evidence" from a notorious crime scene, and a relic of a historic disaster, and I felt I should preserve it. My husband's clothes were in Washington for forensic analysis. Technicians used them to try to calculate the angles and trajectories of the fatal and near-fatal bullets.

Much later I received his clothes in the mail, unpressed and uncleaned, in exactly the same condition as when they had been cut from him at Parkland. I couldn't bear to look at the blood, nor did I feel right about destroying them, so I told the cleaner to remove the stains as best he could but do nothing to alter the holes or other damage, which is exactly what he did.

My pink suit is still in my closet—it would probably still fit if I tried it on. I have no idea what happened to John's suit. Truth be told, I hope I never see it again.

On the other hand, I had kept the little gold cuff link the nurse had given me and used it as a kind of talisman during John's recovery. I called a jeweler in New York, David Webb, who was designing a bracelet for me, and described the cuff link, telling him it contained a little Mexican coin. I said I wanted to preserve it—it was now a family heirloom—but I had no idea how to do it. I knew only I didn't want to wear it around my neck.

The jeweler replied, "Mrs. Connally, we're putting Mexican coins in your new bracelet—a beautiful gold cuff. Why don't we put it there?"

He did; and that's where I wear it to this day.

Such a talisman came in handy when we dealt with the Warren Commission's so-called experts over the coming months. A controversy had arisen due to the fact that several seconds had elapsed between the first shot and the second.

The Commission concluded that John must've been hit by the same bullet that had passed through Kennedy's neck, but we both knew that was impossible. After the first shot, John turned right, then left, then back to center before he was hit. Even "magic" bullets don't hang in the air that long. John heard the first bullet. The second, which hit him, he did not hear—he heard the third. I am told you do not hear a bullet that hits you.

The Zapruder film—an amateur home movie of the shooting whose images are now burned into the American psyche—was our first chance to see what others had witnessed. It was a sickening experience, but strangely surreal, as if it all were happening to someone else at some other time and place. We didn't view it until that trip to Washington, and new details were surfacing left and right.

For example, before then I was unaware that Jackie wasn't holding her husband. Secret Service Agent Clint Hill had climbed onto the trunk as soon as the shooting started and pushed both the Kennedys into the floor of the backseat. I watched the grainy film in disbelief as it showed Jackie crawling onto the trunk. What on earth was she doing? Some said she was trying to escape, to jump from the car and save herself. Others thought it was clear she was trying to help Agent Hill into the vehicle.

When Jackie herself was finally able to talk about the experience, her explanation was absurdly simple—and, given the awful logic of that terrible moment, completely understandable, at least to me.

After the first shot, Jackie was aware that her husband was wounded and in trouble. After the second—the one that mangled my John—she was already moving to help him. After the third, her husband's head had been shattered. Bits of flesh and blood and brain flew everywhere—what felt to me like buckshot and had stung me like hot hail as I bent over John. Jackie said she climbed onto the trunk simply to recover a piece of her husband's skull.

A more stinging criticism of Jackie was that she didn't act to save her husband in time. Analysts claim that if she had reacted immediately and pulled her husband onto her lap after the first shot, he could've lived—the neck wound alone might not have been fatal. But the analysts weren't in the car that day; I was. We were all taken completely off guard. Jackie would've needed superhuman reflexes—and a good dose of precognition—to react in any other way.

Enough has been written about that horrible time, and the Warren Commission itself, to fill a thousand volumes. Suffice it to say that the weight of the evidence we know about convinced both John and me that Oswald—a twenty-four-year-old stock clerk who had been hired a month before to work in the Book Depository—had acted alone: a fact supported by a little investigation we conducted on our own almost ten years later.

When then-President Nixon appointed my husband as secretary of the treasury in 1973, John found himself in charge of our nation's major intelligence branches. With an obvious personal interest in the case and a stake in an unbiased outcome, he pored over every classified document, every memo, every report prepared on the subject. Along with his other duties, he spent months researching every scrap of evidence and found nothing to change his mind. As he said on the twentieth anniversary of the tragedy in 1983, "Nobody in America can keep a secret that big for that long."

More chilling to us personally was the fact that Oswald's dishonorable discharge papers had been signed by none other than Kennedy's then-secretary of the Navy, John Connally. We learned Oswald had written letters protesting that decision, but if his anger had been directed at John, it was misplaced. At the time of Oswald's discharge, my husband was back in Texas, busily campaigning to be its next governor.

We'll never know if Oswald knew his imaginary antagonist was in the same car as the President he hated, but the idea that John might have been a target still sends chills up and down my spine.

As I write these words, forty years after the fact, the assassination of President Kennedy has passed from the realm of law and politics into the world of mythology, so conspiracy theorists will still have their say. But as far as I'm concerned—

as the last living member of the two happy couples who rode in that deadly car—the case is closed, though it cannot be, and never should be, forgotten. ✴

Chapter 13

COPING

Gradually, months of grief gave way to years of reflection.

We seemed to be living the words of Daniel Patrick Moynihan, then a diplomat and later senator from New York, who responded to journalist Mary McGrory's comment that, as a nation facing the aftermath of the assassination, "we would never laugh again." In his inimitable, puckish way, Moynihan replied, "Heavens, Mary—we'll laugh again. It's just that we'll never be young again."

Early in this process, John and I agreed that the assassination would not become our lifelong identity. John believed fervently that his life had been spared for a reason. If that reason was nothing more than to share a few more years with his family, then that would be enough for me, he said.

Although he had a pivotal role in electing three presidents, he could not do the same for himself. He'd overcome a rural background to succeed in state, then national, politics. He'd lived through one of our nation's most horrific times and prevailed. Those accomplishments spoke for themselves. He would not exploit them.

The one fact we couldn't escape was that although men like Oswald are everywhere, President Kennedy *had* been killed in Texas. That stain on our civic pride would take years to erase. We spent many evenings pondering the twists and turns of that fateful visit, wondering if there was any way we could've averted the inevitable:

If only the rain at Love Field had lasted a little longer, the Secret Service would've left the bubble top installed on the President's car, spoiling the assassin's shot.

If only the limousine's standard windows—all bulletproof—had been raised against the wind, there was a chance he would still be alive.

If Jack and Jackie hadn't paused to work the crowd, perhaps we would've passed our sniper earlier and caught him unprepared.

If, if, if.

I even asked John what he thought he was doing when he pushed himself away from me toward the door of the bloody limo when we first arrived at Parkland. He replied that his main concern was for the President: It would be easier for the medics to reach Kennedy if he was out of the way. Terribly wounded though he was, his first thought was to save his friend and commander in chief.

It was all a futile exercise. We might as well have wondered why leaves fall or babies are born. As long as free choice exists in the world, we will have men like Jack Kennedy and Lee Harvey Oswald, and both will act on their beliefs.

John and I were never quite comfortable expressing our private spiritual thoughts to others. Age has made that no easier. But I keep coming back to one idea: God created the heavens and the earth in six days. A lone, and possibly mad, gunman in Dallas remade that universe in six seconds.

We can only wonder what the world would be like if things had been different. I believe Jack Kennedy and John Connally could have achieved great deeds, and moved our country forward. ✦

Chapter 14

THE DISCOVERY

:✦:

So life went on, as it must.

John's term ended and we moved out of the governor's mansion and back to Houston, where he joined a major law firm, Vinson, Elkins, as a partner. But we never fulfilled our dream of living out our years at our ranch, Picosa, in Floresville.

Occasionally I thought about the notes I had written recalling those bitter days in late November 1963, but made no attempt to dig them out and read them. As year piled upon

year I forgot, even, where they were stored.

Thirty-three years later, rummaging through that battered old filing cabinet, I rediscovered my notes. My daughter, Sharon, was with me in Austin when I read them for the first time to a public audience. The event was a luncheon of the Texas State Official Ladies Club. I made no attempt to transcribe them or edit my original work. I just read from the faded pages, rotating the paper as I went so I could follow my tortured handwriting.

After the program, Sharon came up to me and said, "Mother, you sure looked funny reading your notes!"

I blinked in surprise. "Funny? There was nothing in there that was meant to be funny."

"Well, you kept turning your head—up and down and sideways."

"Oh," I laughed, "I was just trying to follow my notes on the edge of the pages!"

I discovered then that Pat Moynihan was right. I had recovered my will to laugh, though the world was no longer young.

I read the notes again a few weeks later at a lecture series sponsored by the Dallas Historical Society. Previous speakers had been bestselling novelist Larry McMurtry, civil war expert Shelby Foote, and Harry Truman biographer David McCullough—a tough group to follow, and certainly way beyond my league as thinkers and speakers. I took the precaution this time of having my notes typed out.

The reading went well enough, but it seems one can never do justice to the dead—especially people you loved. I was startled, therefore, when Dallas journalist Alan Peppard, wrote in a subsequent newspaper:

> *Forget the magic bullet, the grassy knoll, triangulation,*
> *the Cubans, the mob, the CIA, the Warren Commission*

and Oliver Stone. No amount of analysis of the JFK assassination can prepare you for the emotional sledgehammer that comes from hearing the former Texas First Lady, Nellie Connally, quietly read her personal notes describing the scene in the back of that limousine in Dallas, on November 22, 1963 . . . .

In downtown Dallas, the presidential limousine passed through "that great surging, happy crowd," and Mrs. Connally turned and spoke the last words President Kennedy may have ever heard: "Mr. President, you certainly can't say that Dallas doesn't love you." She then heard what she described as "a terrifying noise."

I was very grateful for those kind words, partly because I had accepted the invitation with reservations. I never thought my notes might have any historical significance.

At the request of historians at the University of Texas, the original notes are now stored for safekeeping on campus at the LBJ Library.

My gallant John died in 1993 of pulmonary fibrosis, a disease that involves a scarring of the lungs. He had one good lung and another that had been punctured by slivers of bone when the bullet tore through his chest.

The last photo of us together.

The doctors couldn't say for sure, but it seemed to many that the bullet fired by Lee Harvey Oswald from the same rifle that had killed President John F. Kennedy thirty years before may have claimed its final victim. ✦

Chapter 15

....

UNSPOKEN WORDS

The Nellie Connally Notes

uring the last week in November 1963, I simply could not reconcile the pride and joy I'd felt hosting the Kennedys across Texas with the anger, fear, and confusion that followed the shooting. Like a butterfly on a pin, I was aware only of my pain and knew little of the larger situation or, like everyone else, where all of it would end. My brain just wasn't big enough for all the thoughts and emotions racing through it.

The reflections that follow—faithfully reproduced from the original, now in the archives at the University of Texas— were written a dozen days after the assassination and two days after we left the hospital and returned to Austin. They represent what happened in that car. I didn't record them for history or publication. I knew only that someday my children and grandchildren would want an honest account of what really happened. I wanted them to understand that the Kennedy trip to Texas had been something more than a tragic nightmare.

John F. Kennedy was the first Catholic to occupy the White House, the first President born in the twentieth century, the first American leader to reach into outer space. John and I had shared with the Kennedys the stirrings of friendship, visions of a hopeful future, and moments of great fun. Texans *had* embraced Jack and Jacquelyn Kennedy.

With these thoughts in my mind, I sat down to write for my unborn grandchildren:

THE ASSASSINATION

November 1963

....

I left Austin at noon on Thursday, November 21, 1963. I was excited, I was on my way to San Antonio to meet President and Mrs. John F. Kennedy. John was flying in from Houston and the President was coming in from Washington. I arrived first. There was real excitement in the air. I had a red carpet welcome at the San Antonio airport and went into the terminal where the Vice President and Mrs. Johnson had already arrived and were waiting.

John arrived next and shortly thereafter the big, Air Force 1, the President's jet arrived and the Governor and I and the Vice President and Mrs. Johnson went out to welcome the Kennedy's to Texas. I had never welcomed a President before. I was a little nervous; was my suit all right?

I had presents for the Kennedy's and the Johnson's; watercolors by the San Antonio artist, Onderdonk. Nancy Negley had given me the paintings to present. The door of the plane opened and out stepped Jackie Kennedy in a white dress with black accessories and behind her, the young, handsome, tanned President of the United States. How proud of them I was.

The crowd screamed and cheered. We welcomed them to Texas and off we went and into the President's famous bubble topped car. We sat and started on our first motorcade into Brooks' Medical Center, where the President was to make his first speech in Texas. The crowds were very large, very friendly and screamed, "Mr. President, Jackie," John and Jack waving and smiling all along the long route.

We got out of the car and went into the building, then out on a platform, to face a large crowd. I sat between the Vice President and Eugene Zuckert, Secretary of the Air Force, who introduced the President. He made a fine speech; the crowd was obviously pleased. The ceremonies over...we went back to the cars.

The Governor and I got in the President's car while the Kennedys walked over to another building and we drove around to pick them up. The second car always was a Secret Service car and the third car carried the Vice President and Mrs. Johnson. We drove to the airport, where John and I boarded Air Force 1 to ride with the Kennedy's to Houston, our next stop to attend a dinner honoring Congressman Albert Thomas.

We visited for the short flight in a small sitting room next to the President's bedroom. Mrs. Kennedy stayed with us only a few minutes...(and) retired to the bedroom, but the President stayed and visited with the Governor and Congressman Thomas and several other congressmen flying with us. Senator Ralph Yarborough left the sitting room, because John was there, and rode with the staff forward in the plane.

After landing, we went straight to the hotel to dress for the dinner to be preceded by a brief stop at a LULAC dinner meeting. The President and Mrs. Kennedy arrived just before he was to speak, both looking marvelous. She had on a black theater suit. The crowd was very large and very pleased with our visitors from Washington. Immediately after the dinner we went to the airport...boarded Air Force 1 again and took off for our next stop, Fort Worth.

We arrived after eleven p.m. The crowd at the Carswell Airport was great and the streets at this late hour and in the dark were lined with people all the way from Carswell to the Texas Hotel. The lobby was mobbed...we went straight to our suite, I to bed, the Governor downstairs for coffee and eggs. After all, he was back home for a few hours. So ended Thursday, November 21, 1963.

I awakened early on Friday morning, November 22, 1963. The day was gray and somber. Rain was falling. The parking lot across from the Texas Hotel, where the President would make his first appearance had a small, rain-coated crowd huddled under umbrellas. The small platform was wet. I had a white suit to wear today with black accessories. I was glad I hadn't worn it Thursday or Jackie and I would have looked like twins.

I had two-piece pink wool, with me and decided since the weather was so bad; I would wear it instead of white. John dressed and left for the first appearance with the President.

Someone came for me and we met in a large room close to the grand dining room where a very large, 2,500-to 3,000-person breakfast was to be the President's major activity in Fort Worth.

John had some private words with the President and then the President had some conversation with Senator Yarborough. I make this observation because of rumblings between the Vice President and insults from Senator Yarborough.

The head table, except John, Lyndon and the Congressmen and the Representatives who went with the President and the Kennedys, marched in and were seated. Then all the men came in and only Mrs. Kennedy was among the missing. Everyone was introduced and then, Jackie made a special entrance in a beautiful pink wool suite with navy trim. I had guessed wrong in wearing pink. I never would have if I had known. They loved her, they screamed and yelled and, consumed with curiosity, they stood on their chairs to get a better look at the First Lady of the United States. The President and his Lady were a sight to behold. Youth, charm, vitality, and poise...everyone was pleased.

The President made a great speech in Fort Worth, then out to the cars. This ride, I was put in the car with the Johnson's, since the bubble top car was not used in Fort Worth and only three could sit in the back seat. Senator Yarborough, who had refused to stay in the President's sitting room on the plane with the governor of Texas, and had twice insulted the Vice President of the United States by refusing to ride in the car with him, had been told by the President, in Fort Worth, that he would ride with LBJ or not ride...so he was in the car with us.

I chose to ride in the front with the secret service men and did. The crowds to the airport were friendly...cheering. There were no inappropriate signs, no unpleasantness with the Governor and the Kennedy's. We were on our way to Dallas for a luncheon at the Trade Mart and then off to Austin for a reception at the Governor's Mansion that I had been planning and working on for days.

Was everything in readiness at the Mansion, I wondered? I felt sure I had everything arranged, even down to what the children would wear, but what hostess doesn't have a qualm or two when she is going to entertain a President and First Lady?

The day had changed from a gray, rainy day to a beautiful, bright, sun-shiny day – perfect for a caravan. Before we landed I asked John if I could ride in the car with him in Dallas, he said, "Certainly". When we landed the President's bubble top was being removed and I would have ridden without asking. We got in the jump seats right behind the driver and the secret service man in the front. I was on the driver's side. Mrs. Kennedy got in the back seat directly behind me, and the President sat behind John. The back seat was slightly raised, so that the Kennedy's sat a little higher than we did. John and I were in separate seats with a space between us and were not quite as mobile as Jack and Jackie.

We were indeed a happy foursome, that beautiful morning. I had my yellow roses in my arms and Jackie had her red roses in hers. The crowds were the largest yet and the friendliest. I did so hope Dallas would give the Kennedys a warm and very cordial welcome and I wanted the Kennedys to respond with equal warmth and friendliness. I could not have been more pleased. I felt tingly all over with the pride of a mother whose children are performing just as I had hoped and the relatives were terribly pleased.

We had pleasant banter back and forth between the four of us, but mostly the Kennedys were responding to a rousing ovation, and John and I were just smiling with genuine pleasure that everything was so perfect. We had passed through the downtown area and its great, surging, happy, friendly crowds.

I could resist no longer and turned to the President and said, "Mr. President, you certainly cannot say that Dallas doesn't love you". He smiled in obvious pleasure at the accolades...then I heard a loud, terrifying noise. It came from the back. I turned and looked toward the President just in time to see his hands fly up to his neck and see him sink down in the seat. There was a no utterance of any kind from him. There was no grimace and I had no sure knowledge as to what the noise was.

I felt it was a gunshot and I had a horrifying feeling that the President had not only been shot but could be dead. Quickly, there was a second shot, John had turned to the right at the first shot to look back and then whirled to the left to get another look to see if he could see the President, he could not so he realized the President had been shot. John said, "No, No, No," was hit himself by the second shot and said, "My God, they are going to kill us all," wheeled back to the right, crumpling his shoulders to his knees in the most helpless and pitiful position a tall man could be in.

I reached over and pulled him to me and tried to get us both down in the car. Then came a third shot. With John in my arms, and still trying to stay down, I did not see the third shot hit, but I felt something falling all over me. My sensation was of spent buckshot...my eyes saw bloody matter in tiny bits all over the car. John was bleeding badly all over the front of his shirt.

He was not moving in my arms. I thought my husband was dead. Mrs. Kennedy was saying, "Jack, Jack. They have killed my husband. I have his brains in my hand".

The Secret Service man said to the driver, "pull out of the motorcade," and on his radio phone told the motorcycles preceding us –"to the nearest hospital." We pulled out of the line and drove at a terrific speed toward the nearest hospital. John moved slightly and I knew he was still alive. I started whispering in his ear, "Be still, it's all right, be still, it's all right," all the way to the hospital.

I never looked back after John was shot. But on that terrible, heart- breaking ride I could see the crowds on the right side of the road streaking past, and I couldn't help but think what an awful sight to see, two women holding their lifeless husbands in their arms, streaking down a roadway in utter horror and disbelief. I did not know until later that President and Mrs. Kennedy were in the floor of the car with a Secret Service man on top of them and that I was the only woman holding her dying husband in her arms for the startled people to see.

We made a sharp turn and I almost lost my balance with the heavy weight of my husband, then, almost miraculously, we were at a hospital. The car screeched to a stop. Secret Service men were everywhere. They were crying, "Mr. President," they were begging Mrs. Kennedy to get out of the car. They were crawling all around us, but no one was taking John out of the car. I knew he was alive and, in my heart, I knew the President was dead. I wondered how long I must wait before I could insist that someone tend to my dying husband.

Suddenly, John heaved himself up out of my arms and fell over toward the door. Then some very kind and thoughtful man picked him up in his arms like he was a little baby and put him on a waiting stretcher. They ran off down the strange corridor with him and I ran along behind the stretcher. What I was running from and what I was running to I did not know, but run I must, that much I knew.

The world seemed to be crashing all around me and there was nothing I could do about it. My husband was still living; I knew because he was groaning and saying it hurts as we ran along the short corridor. They took him into a small room on the left and left me standing, as alone as I have ever been, outside a closed door.

There was much confusion behind me and they were wheeling President Kennedy into the room on the right just across from John. The hall was full of Secret Service men, nurses, doctors. Someone brought two straight-backed chairs, one for Mrs. Kennedy and one for me. They were placed immediately outside the emergency room doors, the bullet-ridden bodies of our husbands on the other side.

Someone rushed up to me and said I would have to go to the office and fill out an information blank on John. How totally incongruous, I thought. I did not budge.

Mayor Earl Cabell, of Dallas, appeared and asked me if there was anything he could do for me. I was, even at that strangely unreal time, so grateful for a friend. John's assistant, Bill Stinson, traveling with us on the tour, had been a few cars behind and had now reached Emergency Room 2. A masked nurse or doctor brought me one gold cuff link. I looked in the room and saw John pale, but moving on the table.

Mr. Stinson came out and said my husband had said to him, "please take care of Nellie". Could anything nicer happen to a wife than to have her husband in that pathetic shot up, half conscious state, think of her concerns and welfare? He is a remarkable and so very wonderful man. That one statement would sustain me now and could if need be comfort me forever.

The unreal horror of the hallway in Parkland Hospital outside Emergency Room 1 and Emergency Room 2 is indescribable—doctors, nurses, hospital personnel, Secret Service, machine guns, strange faces and occasionally a familiar face. Mrs. Kennedy, knowing her husband was dead...me, wondering, how long could my husband live? Several times I got out of my chair and pushed open the door to Emergency Room 2 to see for myself if John was still with me. A groan, the twitch of a foot would momentarily satisfy me. I wondered too, did they have adequate and good doctors tending John or were they all across the hall with the President?

Suddenly, they wheeled my husband out of the emergency room and someone said they were taking him to surgery. Again, not knowing my destination, I ran after a stretcher bearing the struggling to live body of my husband down strange corridors. Then I waited a lifetime, an eternity for the certain news of life or death. There had been hope up to now in the unknown, actual knowledge was to be so very sure!

An earlier fear was to be alleviated soon. A very kind and excellent thoracic surgeon, Dr. Robert Shaw, was explaining the terrible wound in the chest. Bill Stinson was in the operating room and was sent several times to me by Dr. Shaw with reassuring information during the very long operation. The wound was not as bad as anticipated. Miraculously, the bullet had missed fatal arteries.

The pierced lung was repaired; the sliced out rib

would eventually take care of itself. My husband, barring complications and helped by a wonderful physical condition, plus his strong will, would live. We were almost sure. The path of the bullet was explained to me. It entered his right shoulder, took out five inches of his 5th rib, pierced his lung and exited just below the right nipple of his chest. (It passed through his right wrist and lodged in his left leg.)

Members of our families and friends began to arrive at the hospital while John was in surgery. My sister, Sheba, and her husband, Bill Bryant, got to me very quickly from Sherman. John's brother, Merrill Connally, and his wife Mary were among the first and since the four of us are so very close, it was comforting to have them as always by our sides. John Singleton from Houston, John's mother and sister from Dallas, Adele Locke from Dallas, the Cassidys and the Strauss'.

In the corridor outside Emergency Room 1, I thought of the children, John, Sharon and Mark. I knew I had to get word to them as soon as I could. What word could I give them? I asked that they be called in Austin and told that their father was alive because I had no way of knowing what sort of reports they were getting.

I knew the assassination of a President and the ascension of a new President might leave the news of a wounded Governor little air time. It later proved I had been correct. There was little news of John Connally and what there was,

was incorrect; three wounds in the head...several chest wounds...The Governor was dead!

I later learned that the children had behaved, as I knew they would with all the self-control we would have hoped for. They were all in school, three separate schools. They were each informed by someone at their schools and picked up by Mansion guards and taken to the Governor's Mansion, where they stayed by the phone, radio and television until they received direct word from me.

Their schools had informed us that we could be very proud of their behavior at a time when self-control came so very hard. My mother, Mrs. Arno (Katie) Brill, went immediately to the Mansion and stayed with them through the long days and nights that were to follow until we returned home.

As soon as I knew that John would live, I called the children. They, of course, wanted to come immediately to Dallas. I asked them to stay in Austin and when their Daddy could see and talk to them I would have them brought to us. Mark and Sharon were content enough, with the knowledge that John would be all right, to remain in Austin, but not our oldest, John III, who came that very day to Parkland Hospital and stayed with me to watch for himself the progress of his father.

John was taken from surgery to the recovery room, a large L-shaped room with six to eight beds, depending on how many were needed. I was given a little cell-like room with no window, a door leading to the hall and door leading into the recovery room. I could walk through that door and have a look myself at John whenever I felt the need. We had been placed under strict security. The entire hospital had.

There was a guard outside both my doors, two in the recovery room and how many about the hospital I never knew. They were all over the corridors. When I first went in the recovery room to see John it was a truly shocking sight. I was not prepared for what I saw, tubes in his right leg, tubes in his left arm, tubes out of both front and back chest, his arm suspended from a sling, an oxygen mask over his face. My legs were weak and trembly, my stomach was so queasy, I felt faint and yet, I was so grateful and so relieved that I had enough strength to approach his bedside, kiss him on the cheek and talk very quietly and briefly to him.

This was a moment of real meaning for John and me. We had experienced such a terrible tragedy…we were so glad to be alive, to have each other, to have been spared for what reason, we did not know. Even in a severe state of shock, we knew for this one precious moment how lucky we were. One of the first things he said was, "This is _____", and he introduced me, Merrill and Julian Read to his nurse.

John asked about the President, but the question was evaded, after counsel with his Doctors, it was decided not to tell him that day about the President. Maybe tomorrow when he was better. Saturday morning he asked me about the President again and I answered, "the President is dead." His reply was soft and sad, "I knew," he said. There followed long days and sleepless nights for me. I slept so little the first night, maybe an hour — maybe two. Each time I tried, the nightmare of the assassination would race through my memory again and again, over and over. It was all I could think about, all I could talk about. What if? Why, Why, Why?

The second and third night in my little cell I had a very mild sleeping pill. I never take them, but my body was so weary and my mind so overworked that I needed some rest. I slept four to five hours both nights. Everyone was so good to us; the hospital couldn't have been more thoughtful and helpful. The Governor's office was set up in the hospital. Flowers, telegrams, letters came pouring in by the hundreds.

While we were still in the recovery room, Jack Ruby shot Oswald and they brought him to the very hospital in which my husband was very slowly and laboriously recovering from the gunshot wound he had given him. Oswald died. The security was strengthened around the hospital. They talked of moving John to private rooms. I was not willing as long as he needed all the suction and equipment and other things so handy in the recovery room. I wanted whatever he needed to be close at hand and not have to be brought in from down the hall.

By now, the thought I had outside Emergency Room 1 that maybe John did not have the best doctors — was long gone! I knew he had the very best doctors to be had anywhere. What they had done for John — and not just for him — for me,

John, Sharon and Mark had proved to me they were the best in the world. They have my devotion always.

I stayed all day Friday, November 22, in my pink suit, blood streaked and rumpled. I had very few things with me, three suits and a cocktail dress. Adele Locke brought me her clothes, dresses, robes, nightgowns, shoes. I changed clothes, I ate, I read mail, I watched television, I went in to have another look at John. I talked with his aides. I visited with Mary Connally, Sheba, Nancy Sayers, Adele Locke.

Days and nights came and went. My mind was never still. I didn't cry or scream or sob. I was not hysterical. I was scared, cautious, suspicious. I was living in an unnatural state for me. For the first time in my life, I was afraid for my family!

People were not satisfied with the reports concerning the recuperation of the Governor. The doctors, (and two of John's aides) Julian Read, and George Christian, were giving medical reports constantly. The press was not satisfied. The people of Texas were not sure. I was asked to make a television statement, knowing everyone would be sure that I was giving them the truth. I had made no statements. I had many requests. I knew I had participated in a tragic moment in history. I had heard and seen so much.

Until the proper authorities had questioned me, I decided to make no statements of any sort. This was different, however, and after first saying, no, I decided maybe I could. I agreed, only if I could read my statement and not be asked questions. I was terribly concerned for Mrs. Tippit, whose husband had been killed trying to stop Oswald. I had a request to make for her and a brief statement about Dallas that I wanted to make. I had not accounted for the emotional strain of making my statement.

It was perhaps one of the most difficult things I've ever had to do. I could neither hold my paper nor read it. So, I put it on the table before me, put on my glasses and read my prepared statement. I had such a strong feeling about how warmly Dallas had received the Kennedys that I felt the need to tell that to the television audience, not only in Texas, but all over the United States and wherever the telecast might go. I removed my glasses and made my plea for a city that was taking too much abuse for something it did not do:

"The governor is now apparently out of danger," I began. *"He asked me to tell everyone he is going to be all right. John had a very, very close call. We thank God he was spared.*

"The governor is in good spirits and we are deeply appreciative of the care he has received at Parkland Hospital from the doctors, the nurses and the staff.

"Governor Connally has asked me to convey to the people of Texas, the nation and the world our deep sorrow over the tragedy which struck at one of President Kennedy's most triumphant hours. Words cannot fully express to Mrs. Kennedy and to the President's family our feelings, which we

know all Texans share.

"Our son, John, will be our personal representative at the funeral of the President in Washington on Monday. The governor joins me in asking that all Texans observe the day of mourning in memory of the President."

I asked that well wishers send a donation to the family of Officer J. D. Tippett, who was shot to death trying to arrest Lee Harvey Oswald, rather than continue sending flowers and gifts to the hospital. Then I looked up from my statement and added, quietly:

"We had been with the President and Mrs. Kennedy during the tour. It had been a wonderful tour and when we arrived in Dallas, and were in the motorcade, the people could not have been friendlier, the crowd more wonderful or more generous in their reaction to the President. The city of Dallas does not deserve to be blamed for this ghastly crime."

I went straight back to my little window-less room, adjoining John's room, to be sure he was all right. ✴

I left Austin at noon on Thursday Nov 21, 1963. I was excited - I was on my way to San Antonio to meet President and Mrs. John F. Kennedy. John was flying in from Houston and the President was coming in from Washington. I arrived first - there was real excitement in the air - I had a red carpet welcome at the S.A. airport & went into the Terminal where the Vice Pres & Mrs. Johnson had already arrived & were waiting. John arrived next & shortly thereafter the big Air Force 1 - the President's jet arrived & the Governor & I & Mr. & Mrs. Johnson went out to welcome the Kennedys to Texas. I had never welcomed a President before - I was a little nervous - was my slip all right - I had presents for the Kennedys & the Johnsons - watercolors by the San Antonio artist Lunderdook (Warren Hegley had given me the painting to present) The door of the plane opened & out stepped Jackie Kennedy in a white dress with black accents and behind her the young, handsome, tanned President of the United States. How proud of them I was - The crowd screamed and cheered - we welcomed them to Texas & off we went and into the President famous bubble topped car we got and started on our first Motorcade un to Brooks Medical Center where the President was to make his first speech in Texas. The crowds were very large. Very friendly and screamed Mr President - Jackie - John + Jack waving and smiling all along the ___ mile route -

We got out of the Car + went in to the building then out on a plat form to face a crowd of about ___ people. I sat between the Vice President and Eugene Zuckert, Secretary of Air Force who introduced the President. He made a fine speech - the crowd was obviously pleased. The ceremonies over we went back to the Cars. The Gov + I got in the President's Car While they walked over to another building + we drove around to pick them up. The second Car always was a Secret service Car + the third Car carried the Vice Pres + Mrs. J. We drove to the Airport where John + I boarded Air Force 1 to ride with the Kennedys to Houston our next stop to attend a dinner honoring Cong. Albert Thomas.

We rested for the short flight in a small sitting room next to the President's bed room. Mrs. Kennedy stayed with us only a few minutes retired to the bed room but the President stayed & visited with the Gov & Cong Thomas & several other Congressmen flying with us. After landing we went straight to the hotel to dress for the dinner & to be preceded by a long stop at a Ladies dinner meeting. The President & Mrs. Kennedy arrived just before he was to speak. Looking marvelous. She had on a black theater suit. The crowd was very large and very pleased with our visitors from Washington. Immediately after the dinner we went to the airport - boarded Air Force 1 again & took off for our next stop Fort Worth. We arrived after eleven P.M. - The crowd at the airport was great and the streets at this late hour & in the dark were lined with people all the way from Carswell to the Texas Hotel. The lobby was mobbed - we went straight to our suite - I to bed - the Gov went downstairs for coffee & eggs and after all he was back home for a few hours. So ended Thursday November 21 1963.

I awakened early on Friday morning – November 22, 1963. The day was gray & somber. Rain was falling. The parking lot across from the Hotel where the President would make his first appearance had a small rain coated crowd huddled under umbrellas. The travel plat form was wet. I had a white suit to wear today with black accessories. I was glad I hadn't worn it Thursday as Jackie & I would have looked like twins. I had a two piece pink wool with me decided since the weather was so bad – I would wear it instead of white. John arrived & left for the first appearance with the President. Some one came for me & we met in a large room close to the great dining room where a very large – 2500 – 3000 person breakfast was to be the President's major activity in Fort Worth. The head table except for John Lyndon & the Kennedys marched in & were seated. Then all the men came in & only Mrs Kennedy was among the missing. Everyone was introduced & then Jackie made a special entrance in a beautiful pink wool suit with Navy trim. I had general envy in wearing pink

Consumed with Curiosity

I never would have if I had known. They loved her—screamed & queened & they stood on their chairs to get a better look at the First Lady of the United States. The President and his Lady were so swept & honored. Youth, charm—vitality—poise—everyone was pleased. The President made a great speech in Fort Worth—then out to the cars—This time I was put in the car with the Johnsons since the bubble top car was not used in Fort Worth & only 3 could sit in the back seat. Senator Yarborough had refused to stay in the President's sitting room on the plane with the Gov & Lady—and had twice insulted the Vice President of the U.S. by refusing to ride in the car with him. He had been told by the President in Ft Worth that he would ride with LBJ so he was in the car with us. I chose to ride in the front with the secret service men & did. The crowds to the airport were friendly—cheering. There were no unappropriate signs—no unpleasant ones along the miles & caravans & carousel where I was put on his force! with the Gov and the Kennedys. We were on our way to Dallas for a luncheon at the Trade Mart & then off to Austin for a reception at the Governors Mansion that I had been planning & working on for days— was everything in readiness at the Mansion? I worried. I felt sure— I had had everything arranged even down to what the children would wear— but what hostess doesn't have a qualm or two when she is to entertain a President and the First Lady?

The day had changed from a gray rainy day to a beautiful cool, bright sunshiny day— perfect for a ceremony. Before we landed I asked John if I could ride in the car with him in Dallas. He said, "Certainly". When we landed the Presidents Bubbletop was there & I would have ridden without asking. We got in the jump seats right behind the driver & the secret service man in the front. I was on the drivers side. Mrs. Kennedy got in the back seat directly behind me & the President sat behind John. The back seat was slightly raised so that the occupants sat a little higher than us. John & I were in separate seats with a space between us. + were not quite as mobile as Jack & Jackie. We were indeed a happy foursome that bright morning. I had my yellow roses in my arms & Jackie had her red roses in hers. The crowds were the largest yet & the friendliest. I did so hope Dallas would give the Kennedys a warm & merry cordial welcome & I wanted the Kennedys to respond with equal warmth & friendliness. I could not have been more pleased. I felt tingly all over with the pride of a mother whose children are performing just as I had hoped & the spectators were terribly pleased. We had pleasant banter back & forth between the 4 of us but mostly the Kennedys were responding to a roaring ovation & John & I were just smiling with genuine pleasure that everything was so perfect. We had passed through the downtown area and its great surging happy friendly crowds. I could resist no longer & turned to the President & said "Mr. President, you certainly cannot say that Dallas doesn't love you." — He smiled in obvious pleasure at the accolades — then I heard a loud terrifying noise. It came from the back. I turned & looked toward the President just in time to see him clutch his neck & sink down in the seat. There was no utterance of any kind from him. There was no scream. I had

no sure knowledge as to what the noise
was. I felt it was a gunshot & I
had a horrifying feeling that the
President had not only been shot
but could be dead. Quickly there was a
second shot (John had turned to the
right at the first shot & look back
& had then wheeled to the left to get
another look & realized the President
had been shot and "No, no, no")
was hit very hard and said, My God, they are
going to kill us all I wheeled back
& the right crumpling his shoulders
& his knees in the most helpless &
pitiful position a tall big man
can be in. I reached over &
pulled him to me & tried to get us
both down in the car. There
came a third shot. With John
in my arms & still trying to stay
down I did not see the third
shot hit — but I felt something
falling all over me. My sensation
was I spent buckshot — my
eyes saw bloody matter in tiny bits
all over the car. John was bleeding
badly all over the front of his shirt

*to me
the Pres.
he could
not
so he

— on that unbearable helpless ride —

He was not moving in my arms.
I thought my husband was dead.
Mrs. Kennedy was saying "Jack, Jack
they have killed my husband. I
have his brains in my hand."

The secret service men said to the
Driver — Pull out of the Motor Cade &
on his radio phone told the Motor
cycle & preceding us — to the nearest
hospital. We pulled out of the line
& drove at a terrific speed toward
the nearest hospital. John moved
slightly & I knew he was still alive
I started whispering in his ear. "Be still —
It's alright. Be still. It's alright — all
the way to the Hospital. I never could
keep up after John was shot — but on
that terrible heartbreaking ride I could
see the crowd on the right
side of the road flashing past & I couldn't
keep but think what an awful
sight to see two women holding their
legless husbands in their arms streaking
down a road way in utter horror
& disbelief *We make a sharp turn and
I almost lost my balance with the
heavy weight of my husband — then

(10)

almost miraculously we were at a hospital. The car screeched to a stop. Secret Service men were everywhere. They were crying. "Mr. President" — They were begging Mrs. Kennedy to get out of the car. They were crowding all around us but no one was taking John out of the car. I knew he was alone and in my heart I knew the President was dead. I wondered how long I must wait before I could insist that someone tend to my dying husband. Suddenly John heaved himself up out of my arms & fell over toward the door. Then some very kind and thoughtful man picked him up in his arms like he was a little baby & put him on a bent thing stretcher — They ran off down the corridor with him & I ran along behind the stretcher. What I was running from & what I was running to I did not know — but run I must — that much I knew.

(11)

They would seemed to be crashing all around me, and there was nothing I could do about it. My husband was still living I knew, because he was groaning and trying — It hurts to see him so along the short corridor. They took him into a small room on the left as alone as I've ever been and left me standing outside a closed door. There was much confusion behind me and they were wheeling President Kennedy into the room on the right just across from John. The hall was full of secret Service men — nurses & doctors. Someone brought two straight backed chairs one for Mrs. Kennedy + one for me — they were placed immediately outside the emergency room doors. the bullet ridden bodies of our husbands on the other side. Some one rushed up to me and said I would have to go to the office and fill out an information blank on John. How totally incongruous — I thought. I did not budge.

⟨4⟩

8 Drms

Mayor Cahill appeared and
asked me if there was anything
he could do for me. I [said], even
at that strangely unreal time, so
grateful for a friend. John's headrest
Bull Sterson, travelling with us in
the town had been [x] for cars
behind & had now reached the
emergency room 2 — a [nurse/trusted?]
brought me one gold cufflink —
I looked in the room — & saw
John pale but moving on the
table — Mr. Stinson came and &
said My husband had said to
him — "Please take care of Nellie" —
Could anything nicer happen to
a niece than to have her husband
in the politics shut up half
conscious state — think of her ⟨concern &⟩
welfare. He is a remarkable and
so very wonderful man. That one
Statement would sustain me now
and could if need be comfort me
forever.

ⓐ Dicta.

(13)

The unreal horror of the hall-way in Parkland Hospital out side Emergency room 1 & Emergency room 2 is indescribable. Doctors — nurses — hospital personnel — secret service — machine guns — strange faces — occasionally a familiar face — Mrs. Kennedy knowing her husband was dead — Me — wondering how long my husband could live. Several times I got out of my chair & pushed open the door to Emergency room 2 & see for myself if John ~~still~~ was still alive me. A groan — the twitch of a foot would momentarily satisfy me. I wondered too — and they have adequate and good doctors tending John or were they all across the hall with ~~out~~ the President. Suddenly they wheeled my husband out of the Emergency room & Takes him to surgery — again not knowing my destination — I ran after a stretcher bearing the "struggling" (unsure) body of my husband down strange corridors — There I waited — a lifetime an eternity for the ~~cliffhanger~~ verdict of life or death. There had been hope deep & now in the unknown — Actual knowledge was to be so very sure!

Our earlier fears were to be alleviated
soon - a very kind and excellent
thoracic surgeon, Dr. ___ Shaw was
explaining the terrible wound in the
~~badly damaged~~ chest. But Stearns
was in the operating room and was
sent several times to me by Dr. Shaw
with reassuring information during
this very long operation. The wound
was not as bad as anticipated -
miraculously the bullet had missed
fatal arteries - the pierced lung was
repaired - the places out risk - could
eventually take care of it say. My husband
barring complications & helped by
a wonderful physical condition plus
his strong will would live - We
were almost sure. The path of the
bullet was explained to me. It entered
his right shoulder took out 5 inches
of his 5th (?) rib - pierced his lung
and exited just below the right
nipple of his chest.
    Members of our families and
friends had begun to arrive at the
hospital while he was in surgery -

15

* From Floresville Judge

John's brother, Merrill Connally & his wife Mary were among the first & since the four of us are so very close it was comforting to have them as always by our side.

* (My sister - Sheba took off & her husband, Bud Bryant got to me very quickly from Sherman.)

John Singleton from Houston - John's brothers & sisters from Dallas - Aace Luke from Dallas - the Connally & Stans.

In the corridor outside Emergency Room I I thought of the children John, Sharon & Mark. I knew I had to get word to them as soon as I could. What word could I give them — I asked that they be called in Austin and told that their father was alive because I had no way of knowing what sort of reports they were getting. I knew the assassination of a President and the swearing in of a new President might leave the news of a wounded Governor little air time. It later proved- I had been correct — there was little news of John Connally & what there was was incorrect. Three wounds in the head — Several chest wounds — The Governor was dead. — I later

NELLIE CONNALLY   171

learned that the children had behaved
as I knew they would with all
the self control we would have
hoped for. They were all in School. — 3
separate Schools — they were each
informed by someone at their Schools
& picked up by Missouri Guards
and taken to the Governors Mansion
where they stayed by phone, radio &
television until they received
direct word from me. We have been
informed by their Schools that
we could be very proud of their
behavior at a time when self
control ~~comes~~ so very hard.

My mother, Mrs. Amo Brill, went immediately to
the Mansion and stayed with them
through the ~~entire~~ long days and
nights that were to follow until
we returned home.

As soon as I knew that John would
live — I called the children. They of
course, wanted to come immediately
to Dallas. I asked them to stay in
Austin & when their Daddy could
see & talk to them I would have
them brought to us. Mark & Sharon

17

were content enough on the knowledge that John would be alright to remain in Austin — but John who came that very day to Parkland Hospital & stayed with me & watch for himself the progress of his father.

John was taken from surgery to the recovery room — a large L shaped room with — 6-8 beds depending on how many were needed. I was in a little cell like room with no window a door leading to the hall & a door leading into the recovery room. I could walk thru that door & have a look myself at John whenever I felt the need. We had been placed under strict security — the entire hospital had. There was a guard outside both my doors — two in the recovery room & how many about the hospital I never knew. They were all over the corridors — When I first went in the recovery room I saw John it was a truly shocking sight. I was not prepared for what I saw — tubes in his right leg — tubes in his left arm — tubes out of his front & back chest — his arm suspended from a sling — an oxygen mask over his face — My legs were weak & trembling — my stomach was

so queasy – I felt faint and yet –
I was so grateful and so relieved
that I had enough strength to
approach his bedside – kiss him on
the cheek and talk very quietly and
briefly to him. This was a Moment of real
meaning for John & me. We had experienced
such a terrible Tragedy – we were so
~~grateful~~ glad to be alive – to have each
other – to have been spared for
what reason – we did not know.
Even in a severe State of Shock – we
knew for this one precious moment how
lucky we were. ✳ John asked about
the President – but the question was
evaded – after consultation with his Doctors
it was decided not to tell him that
day about the President. Maybe tomorrow
when he was better. Saturday morning.
he asked me about the President again & I
answered. "The President is dead" – His reply
was soft and sad "I knew" – he said!
There followed ~~long~~ and sleepless nights
for me. I slept so little the first night –
maybe an hour – maybe two – each time
I tried the night nurse J the accident would
race thru my memory again & again
over & over – It was all I could think
about all I can is talk about – why –
why – why why why – The second & third
night in my own cell I had a very mild

✳ One of the first things he
said – This is [illegible] and I [illegible] of John her

sleeping pill — I never take them—but my body was so weary & my mind so overworked that I needed some rest — I slept 4 or 5 hours each night. Everyone was so good to us — the hospital couldn't have been more thoughtful & helpful. The governess office was set up in the hospital — flowers - Telegrams - letters — came pouring in by the hundreds —

While we were still in the recovery room Ruby shot Oswald & they brought him to the very hospital in which my husband was very slowly & laboriously recovering from the gunshot wound he had given him. Oswald died — the security was strengthened around the hospital. They talked of moving John D private rooms — I was against willing as long as he needed all the outside equipment & other things to have the recovery room. I wanted whatever he needed & he close at hand & not have to be brought in from down the hall.

By now the thought I had had outside emergency room ! that maybe he did not have the best doctors — was long gone. I knew he had had the very best doctors & he had anywhere. What they had done for John — & for him — for me

John, Sharon + Mark, had proved to me — they were the best in the world. They have my gratitude and devotion always

I stayed all day Thursday - November 22 in my pink suit — blood streaked and rumpled. I had very few things with me. — 3 suits and a first aid dress Aunt Lorise brought me her clothes — dresses — robes — night gowns. Shoes — some one took the 2nd pink suit & had it cleaned — I changed clothes — I ate — I read mail — I watched television — I went in to have another look at John — I talked with his aides — I visited with Mary Connally — Sheba — Nancy Joyers — Adele Locke days & nights came & went — my mind was never still — I didn't cry — or scream — or sob — I was not hysterical — I was scared — I was Cautious — I became Suspicious — I was living in an unnatural state for me — for the first time in my life I was afraid for my family

People there not satisfied with the reports concerning the recuperation of the Governor. The Doctors — Julian Read + George Christian were giving medical reports constantly — the press was not satisfied — the people of Texas were not sure — I was asked to make a television statement knowing everyone would be sure that I was giving them the truth. I had made no statement — I had had many requests — I knew I had participated in a tragic moment in history — I had heard & seen so much — (until I had been questioned by the proper authorities) I decided I'd make no statement of any sort. This was different however and after first saying no — I decided maybe I could! I suddenly thought I could read my statement and not be asked questions. I was terribly concerned for Mrs. Tippett whose husband had been killed trying to stop Oswald — I had a request to make for her and a brief statement about Dallas that I wanted to make. Still I had not accounted for the emotional strain of making my statement. It was perhaps one of the most difficult things I've ever had to do. I could neither hold my paper nor read it — So I put it on the table before me — put on my glasses & read my prepared statement — I had such a strong feeling about how warmly Dallas had received the Kennedys that I felt the need to tell that too to the television audience not only in Texas but all over the United States & wherever the

the telecast night go. I removed my glasses & made a one [crossed out] plea for "city" that was taking too much abuse for something it did not do. I said ("

Insert statement)   If you can find statement

I was instructed to reach the breaking point as I read the words. Each sentence became louder — finally it was done — now I could make my request for Mrs. Tippit and my personal reaction to Dallas' greeting of the Kennedys

I went straight back to my little windowless room — straight on to be sure John was alright
Nellie Connally

We Are . . . The Watchmen
on the Walls of Freedom

....

T HE FOLLOWING IS THE TEXT OF THE SPEECH
President John Fitzgerald Kennedy was
scheduled to deliver in the Trade Mart at
Dallas, Texas, at noon on November 22, 1963:

I am honored to have this invitation to address the annual
meeting of the Dallas Citizens Council, joined by members of
the Dallas Assembly—and pleased to have this opportunity
to salute the Graduate Research Center of the Southwest.

It is fitting that these two symbols of Dallas's progress are
united in the sponsorship of this meeting. For they represent
the best qualities, I am told, of leadership and learning in this
city—and leadership and learning are indispensable to each
other. The advancement of learning depends on community
leadership for financial support—and the products of that
learning, in turn, are essential to the leadership's hopes for
continued progress and prosperity. It is not a coincidence
that those communities possessing the best in research and
graduate facilities—from MIT to Cal Tech—tend to attract

"WE ARE . . . THE WATCHMEN ON THE WALLS OF FREEDOM"

The text of the speech President John Fitzgerald Kennedy
was scheduled to deliver in the Trade Mart in Dallas, Texas,
at noon on November 22, 1963.

the new and growing industries. I congratulate those of you here in Dallas who have recognized these basic facts through the creation of the unique and forward-looking Graduate Research Center.

This link between leadership and learning is not only essential at the community level. It is even more indispensable in world affairs. Ignorance and misinformation can handicap the progress of a city or a company—but they can, if allowed to prevail in foreign policy, handicap this country's security. In a world of complex and continuing problems, in a world full of frustrations and irritations, America's leadership must be guided by the lights of learning and reason—or else those who confuse rhetoric with reality and the plausible with the possible will gain the popular ascendancy with their seemingly swift and simple solutions in every world problem.

There will always be dissident voices heard in the land, expressing opposition without alternatives, finding fault but never favor, perceiving gloom on every side and seeking influence without responsibility. Those voices are inevitable.

But today other voices are heard in the land—voices preaching doctrines wholly unrelated to reality, wholly unsuited to the sixties, doctrines which apparently assume that words will suffice without weapons, that vituperation is as good as victory and that peace is a sign of weakness. At a time when the national debt is steadily being reduced in terms of its burden on our economy, they see that debt as the greatest single threat to our security. At a time when we are steadily reducing the number of federal employees serving every thousand citizens, they fear those supposed hordes of servants far more than the actual hordes of opposing armies.

We cannot expect that everyone, to use the phrase of a decade ago, will "talk sense to the American people." But we can hope that fewer people will listen to nonsense. And the notion that this nation is headed for defeat through deficit, or that strength is but a matter of slogans, is nothing but just plain nonsense.

I want to discuss with you today the status of our strength and our security because this question clearly calls for the most responsible qualities of leadership and the most enlightened products of scholarship. For this nation's strength and security are not easily or cheaply obtained, nor are they quickly and simply explained. There are many kinds of strength and no one kind will suffice. Overwhelming nuclear strength cannot stop a guerrilla war. Formal pacts of alliance cannot stop internal subversion, displays of material wealth cannot stop the disillusionment of diplomats subjected to discrimination. Above all, words alone are not enough. The United States is a peaceful nation. And where our strength and determination are clear, our words need merely to convey conviction, not belligerence. If we are strong, our strength will speak for itself. If we are weak, words will be of no help.

I realize that this nation often tends to identify turning points in world affairs with the major addresses which preceded them. But it was not the Monroe Doctrine that kept all Europe away from this hemisphere—it was the strength of the British fleet and the width of the Atlantic Ocean. It was not General Marshall's speech at Harvard which kept Communism out of Western Europe—it was the strength and stability made possible by our military and economic assistance.

In this administration also it has been necessary at times to issue specific warnings—warnings that we could not stand by and watch the Communists conquer Laos by force, or intervene in the Congo, or swallow West Berlin or maintain offensive missiles on Cuba. But while our goals were at least temporarily obtained in those and other instances, our successful defense of freedom was due—not to the words we used—but to the strength we stood ready to use on behalf of the principles we stand ready to defend.

This strength is composed of many different elements, ranging from the most massive deterrents to the most subtle influences. And all types of strength are needed—no one kind could do the job alone. Let us take a moment, therefore, to review this nation's progress in each major area of strength.

First, as Secretary McNamara made clear in his address last Monday, the strategic nuclear power of the United States has been so greatly modernized and expanded in the last 1,000 days, by the rapid production and deployment of the most modern missile systems, that any and all potential aggressors are clearly confronted now with the impossibility of strategic victory—and the certainty of total destruction—if by reckless attack they should ever force upon us the necessity of a strategic reply.

In less than three years, we have increased by 50 percent the number of Polaris submarines scheduled to be in force by the next fiscal year—increased by more than 70 percent our total Polaris purchase program—increased by more than 75 percent the portion of our strategic bombers on 15-minute alert—and increased by 100 percent the total number of nuclear weapons available in our strategic alert forces. Our security is further enhanced by the steps we have taken regarding these weapons to improve the speed and certainty of their response, their readiness at all times to respond, their ability to attack and survive an attack and their ability to be carefully controlled and directed through secure command operations.

But the lessons of the last decade have taught us that freedom cannot be defended by strategic nuclear power alone. We have, therefore, in the last three years accelerated the development and deployment of tactical nuclear weapons—increased by 60 percent the tactical nuclear forces deployed in Western Europe.

Nor can Europe or any continent rely on nuclear forces alone, whether they are strategic or tactical. We have radically improved the readiness of our conventional forces—increased by 100 percent the procurement of modern army weapons and equipment—increased by 100 percent our ship construction, conversion and modernization program—increased by 100 percent our procurement of tactical air squadrons—and increased the strength of the Marines. As last month's "Operation Big Lift"—which originated here in Texas—showed so clearly, this nation is prepared as never before to move substantial numbers of men in surprisingly little time to advanced positions anywhere in the world. We have increased by 175 percent the procurement of airlift aircraft—and we have already achieved a 75 percent increase in our existing strategic airlift capability.

Finally, moving beyond the traditional roles of our military forces, we have achieved an increase of nearly 600 percent in our special forces—those forces that are prepared to work with our allies and friends against the guerrillas, saboteurs, insurgents and assassins who threaten freedom in a less direct but equally dangerous manner.

But American military might should not and need not stand alone against the ambitions of internal Communism. Our security and strength, in the last analysis, directly depend on the security and strength of others—and that is why our military and economic assistance plays such a key role in enabling those who live on the periphery of the Communist world to maintain their independence of choice. Our assistance to these nations can be painful, risky and costly—as is true in Southeast Asia today. But we dare not weary of the task. For our assistance makes possible the stationing of 3.5 million allied troops along the Communist frontier at one-tenth of the cost of maintaining a comparable number of American soldiers. A successful Communist breakthrough in these area, necessitating direct United States intervention, would cost us several times as much as our entire foreign aid program—and might cost us heavily in American lives as well.

About 70 percent of our military assistance goes to nine key countries located on or near the borders of the Communist bloc—nine countries confronted directly or indirectly with the threat of Communist aggression—Viet Nam, Free China, Korea, India, Pakistan, Thailand, Greece, Turkey and Iran. No one of these countries possesses on its own the resources to maintain the forces which our own chiefs of staff think needed in the common interest. Reducing our efforts to train, equip and assist their armies can only encourage Communist penetration and require in time the increased overseas deployment of American combat forces. And reducing the economic help needed to bolster these nations that undertake to help defend freedom can have the same disastrous result. In short, the $50 billion we spend each year on our own defense could well be ineffective without the $4 billion required for military and economic assistance.

Our foreign aid program is not growing in size—it is, on the contrary, smaller now than in previous years. It has had its weaknesses—but we have undertaken to correct them—and the proper way of treating weaknesses is to replace them with strength, not to increase those weaknesses by emasculating essential programs. Dollar for dollar, in or out of government, there is no better form of investment in our national security than our much-abused foreign aid program.

We cannot afford to lose it. We can afford to maintain it. We can surely afford, for example, to do as much for our 19 needy neighbors of Latin America as the Communist bloc is sending to the island of Cuba alone.

I have spoken of strength largely in terms of the deterrence and resistance of aggression and attack. But, in today's world, freedom can be lost without a shot being fired, by ballots as well as bullets. The success of our leadership is dependent upon respect for our mission in the world as well as our missiles—on a clearer recognition of the virtues of freedom as well as the evils of tyranny.

That is why our information agency has doubled the shortwave broadcasting power of the Voice of America and increased the number of broadcasting hours by 30 percent—increased Spanish language broadcasting to Cuba and Latin America from one to nine hours a day—increased sevenfold to more than 3.5 million copies the number of American books being translated and published for Latin American readers and taken a host of other steps to carry our message of truth and freedom to all the far corners of the earth.

And that is also why we have regained the initiative in the exploration of outer space—making an annual effort greater than the combined total of all space activities undertaken during the 50s—launching more than 130 vehicles into earth orbit—putting into actual operation valuable weather and communications satellites—and making it clear to all that the United States of America has no intention of finishing second in space.

This effort is expensive, but it pays its own way, for freedom and for America. For there is no longer any fear in the free world that a communist lead in space will become a permanent assertion of supremacy and the basis of military superiority. There is no longer any doubt about the strength and skill of American science, American industry, American education and the American free enterprise system. In short, our national space effort represents a great gain in, and a great resource of, our national strength—and both Texas and Texans are contributing greatly to this strength.

Finally, it should be clear by now that a nation can be no stronger abroad than she is at home. Only an America which practices what it preaches about equal rights and social justice will be respected by those whose choice affects our future. Only an America which has fully educated its citizens is fully capable of tackling the complex problems and perceiving the hidden dangers of the world in which we live. And only an America which is growing and prospering economically can sustain the world-wide defenses of freedom, while demonstrating to all concerned the opportunities of our system and society.

It is clear, therefore, that we are strengthening our security as well as our economy by our recent record increases in national income and output—by surging ahead of most of Western Europe in the rate of business expansion.

And the margin of corporate profits—by maintaining a more stable level of prices than almost any of our overseas competitors—and by cutting personal and corporate income taxes by some $11 billion, as I have proposed, will assure this nation of the longest and strongest expansion in our peacetime history.

This nation's total output—which three years ago was at the $500 billion mark—will soon pass $600 billion, for a record rise of over $100 billion in three years. For the first time in history we have 70 million men and women at work. For the first time in history average factory earnings have exceeded $100 a week. For the first time in history corporation profits after taxes—which have risen 43 percent in less than three years—have reached an annual level of $27.4 billion.

My friends and fellow citizens, I cite these facts and figures to make it clear that America today is stronger than ever before. Our adversaries have not abandoned their ambitions—our dangers have not diminished—our vigilance cannot be relaxed. But now we have the military, the scientific and the economic strength to do whatever must be done for the preservation of our liberty.

That strength will never be used in pursuit of aggressive ambitions—it will always be used in pursuit of peace. It will never be used to promote provocations—it will always be used to promote peaceful settlement of disputes.

We in this country, in this generation, are, by destiny rather than choice, the watchmen on the walls of world freedom. We ask, therefore, that we may be worthy of our power and responsibility—that we may exercise our strength with wisdom and restraint—and that we may achieve in our time and for all time the ancient vision of "peace on earth, good will toward men." That must always be our goal—and the righteousness of our case must always underlie our strength. For as was written long ago: "Except the Lord keep the city, the watchman waketh but in vain." +

THIS COUNTRY IS MOVING . . .
AND IT MUST NOT STOP

....

*T*HE FOLLOWING IS THE TEXT OF THE SPEECH PRESIDENT JOHN FITZGERALD KENNEDY WAS SCHEDULED TO DELIVER AT THE TEXAS WELCOME DINNER AT THE MUNICIPAL AUDITORIUM IN AUSTIN, TEXAS, ON THE EVENING OF NOVEMBER 22, 1963.

One hundred and eighteen years ago last March, President John Tyler signed the joint resolution of Congress providing statehood for Texas. And 118 years ago next month, President James Polk declared that Texas was part of the Union.

Both Tyler and Polk were Democratic presidents, and from that day to this, Texas and the Democratic Party have been linked in an indestructible alliance—an alliance for the promotion of prosperity, growth, and greatness for Texas and for America.

In 1964 that alliance will sweep this state and nation.

The historic bonds that link Texas and the Democratic Party are no temporary union of convenience. They are deeply embedded in the history and purpose of this state and

"THIS COUNTRY IS MOVING . . .
AND IT MUST NOT STOP"

*The text of the speech President John Fitzgerald Kennedy
was scheduled to deliver at the Texas Welcome Dinner at
the Municipal Auditorium in Austin, Texas, on the evening
of November 22, 1963.*

party. The Democratic Party is not a collection of diverse interests brought together only to win elections. We are united instead by a common history and heritage—by a respect for the needs of the past and a recognition of the needs of the future.

Never satisfied with today, we have always staked our fortunes on tomorrow. That is the kind of state Texas has always been—that is the kind of vision and vitality which Texans have always possessed—and that is the reason why Texas will always be basically Democratic.

For 118 years, Texas and the Democratic Party have contributed to each other's success. This state's rise to prosperity and wealth came primarily from the policies and programs of Woodrow Wilson, Franklin Roosevelt and Harry Truman. Those policies were shaped and enacted with the help of such men as the late Sam Rayburn and a host of other key Congressmen—by the former Texas Congressman and Senator who serves now as my strong right arm, Vice President Lyndon B. Johnson—by your present U.S. Senator Ralph Yarborough—and by an overwhelming proportion of Democratic leadership at the state and county level, led by your distinguished Governor, John Connally.

It was the policy and programs of the Democratic Party which helped to bring income to your farmers, industries to your workers and the promotion and presentation of your natural resources.

No one who remembers the days of five-cent cotton and thirty-five cent oil will forget the ties between the success of this state and the success of our party.

Three years ago this fall, I toured this state with Lyndon Johnson, Sam Rayburn and Ralph Yarborough as your party's candidate for President. We pledged to increase America's strength against its enemies, its prestige among its friends, and the opportunities it offered to its citizens. Those pledges have been fulfilled. The words spoken in Texas have been transformed into actions in Washington, and we have America moving again.

Here in Austin, I pledged in 1960 to restore world confidence in the vitality and energy of American society. That pledge has been fulfilled. We have won the respect of allies and adversaries alike through our determined stand on behalf of freedom around the world from West Berlin to Southeast Asia—through our resistance to Communist intervention in the Congo and Communist missiles in Cuba—and through our initiative in attaining the nuclear test ban treaty which can stop pollution of our atmosphere and start us on the path to peace again.

In San Jose and Mexico City, in Bonn and West Berlin, in Rome and County Cork, I saw and heard and felt a new appreciation for America on the move and an America which has shown it cares about the needy of its own and other lands, an America which has shown that freedom is the way to the future, an America which is known to be first in the effort for peace as well as preparedness.

In Amarillo, I pledged in 1960 that the businessmen of this state and nation—particularly the small businessman, who is the backbone of our economy—will move ahead as our economy moved ahead. That pledge has been fulfilled. Business profits—having risen 43 percent in two and one-half years—now stand at a record high; and businessmen all over America are grateful for liberalized depreciation, for the investment tax credit, and for our programs to increase their markets at home as well as abroad.

We have proposed a massive tax reduction, with particular benefits for small business. We have stepped up the activities of the Small Business Administration, making available in the last three years almost $50 million to more than 1,000 Texas firms, doubling their opportunity to share in federal procurement contracts. Our party believes that what is good for American people is good for American business—and the last three years have proven the validity of that proposition.

In Grand Prairie, I pledged in 1960 that this country will no longer tolerate the lowest rate of economic growth of any major industrialized nation in the world. That pledge has been and is being fulfilled. In less than three years our national output will shortly have risen by a record $100 billion—industrial protection is up 22 percent—personal income is up 16 percent. And *The Wall Street Journal* pointed out a short time ago that the United States now leads most of Western Europe in the rate of business expansion and the margin of corporate profits.

Here in Texas, where three years ago, at the very time I was speaking, real per capita personal income was actually declining as the industrial recession spread to this state—more than 200,000 new jobs have been created—unemployment has declined and personal income rose last year to an all-time high. This growth must go on. Those not sharing in this prosperity must be helped. That is why we have an accelerated public works program, an area redevelopment program and a manpower training program—to keep this and other states moving ahead. And that is why we need a tax cut of $11 billion, as an assurance of future growth and as insurance against an early recession. No period of economic recovery in the peacetime history of this nation has been characterized by both the length and strength of our present expansion—and we intend to keep it going.

In Dallas, I pledged in 1960 to step up the development of both our natural and our human resources. That pledge has been fulfilled. The policy of "no new starts" has been reversed. The Canadian River project will provide water for 11 Texas cities. The San Angelo project will irrigate some 10,000 acres. We have launched 10 new watershed projects in Texas, completed seven others and laid plans for six more. A new national park, a new wildlife preserve, and other navigation, reclamation and natural resource projects are all underway in this state. At the same time, we have sought to develop the human resources of Texas and all the nation—granting loans to 17,500 Texas college students—making more than $17 million available to 249 school districts—and expanding or providing rural library service to 600,000 Texas readers. And if this Congress passes, as now seems likely, pending bills to build college classrooms, increase student loans, build medical schools, provide more community libraries, and assist in the creation of graduate centers, then this Congress will have done more for the cause of education than has been done by any Congress in modern history.

Civilization, it was once said, is a race between education and catastrophe—and we intend to win that race by education.

In Wichita Falls, I pledged in 1960 to increase farm income and reduce the burden of farm surpluses. That pledge has been fulfilled. New farm income today is almost a billion dollars higher than in 1960. In Texas, net income per farm consistently averaged below the $4,000 mark during the Benson regime—it is now well above it. And we have raised this income by reducing grain surpluses by 1 billion bushels. We have, at the same time, tackled the problem of the entire rural economy—extending more than twice as much credit to Texas farmers and to the Farmers Home Administration and making more than $100 million in REA loans. We have not solved all the problems of American agriculture—but we have offered hope and a helping hand in place of Mr. Benson's indifference.

In San Antonio, I pledged in 1960 that a new administration would strive to secure for every American his full constitutional rights. That pledge has been and is being fulfilled. We have not yet secured the objectives desired or the legislation required. But we have, in the last three years, by working through voluntary leadership as well as legal action, opened more new doors to members of minority groups—doors to transportation, voting, education, employment and places of public accommodation—than had been opened in any three-year or 30-year period in this century. There is no non-controversial way to fulfill our constitutional pledge to establish justice and promote domestic tranquility—but we intend to fulfill those obligations because they are right.

In Houston, I pledged in 1960 that we would set before the American people the unfinished business of our society. That pledge has been fulfilled. We have undertaken the first full-scale revision of our tax laws in 10 years. We have launched a bold new attack on mental illness, emphasizing treatment in the patient's own home community instead of some vast custodial institution. We have revised our public welfare programs, emphasizing family rehabilitation instead of humiliation, and we have proposed a comprehensive realignment of our national transportation policy, emphasizing equal competition instead of regulation. Our agenda is still long—but this country is moving again.

In El Paso, I pledged in 1960 that we would give the highest and earliest priority to the reestablishment of good relations with the people of Latin America. We are working to fulfill that pledge. An area long neglected has not solved all its problems. The Communist foothold, which had already been established, has not yet been eliminated. But the trend of Communist expansion has been reversed. The name of Fidel Castro is no longer feared or cheered by substantial numbers in every country—and contrary to the prevailing prediction of three years ago, not another inch of Latin American territory has fallen prey to Communist control.

Meanwhile, the work of reform and reconciliation goes on. I can testify from my trips to Mexico, Colombia, Venezuela and Costa Rica that American officials are no longer booed and spat upon South of the Border. Historic fences and friendships are being maintained. And Latin America, once the forgotten stepchild of our aid programs, now receives more economic assistance per capita than any other area of the world. In short, the United States is once more identified with the needs and aspirations of the people to the South—and we intend to meet those needs and aspirations.

In Texarkana, I pledged in 1960 that our country would no longer engage in a lagging space effort. That pledge has been fulfilled. We are not yet first in every field of space endeavor—but we have regained worldwide respect for our scientists, our industry, our education, and our free initiative.

In the last three years, we have increased our annual space effort to a greater degree than the combined total of all space activities undertaken in the 1950s. We have launched into earth orbit more than four times as many space vehicles as had been launched in the previous three years. We have focused our wide-ranging efforts around a landing on the moon in this decade. We have put valuable weather and communications satellites into actual operation. We will fire this December the most powerful rocket ever developed anywhere in the world.

And we have made it clear to all that the United States of America has no intention of finishing second in outer space. Texas will play a major role in this effort. The Manned Space Center in Houston will be the cornerstone of $1 billion already allocated to that center this year. Even though space is an infant industry, more than 3,000 people are already employed in space activities here in Texas—more than $100 million of space contracts are now being worked on in this state—and more than 50 space-related firms have announced the opening of Texas offices. This is still a daring and dangerous frontier, and there are those who would prefer to turn back or to take a more timid stance. But Texans have stood their ground on embattled frontiers before—and I know you will help us see this battle through.

In Fort Worth, I pledged in 1960 to build a national defense that was second to none.

A position, I said, which is not "first, when" but—first, period. That pledge has been fulfilled. In the past few years, we have increased our defense budget by over 20 percent; increased the program for acquisition of Polaris submarines from 24 to 41; increased our Minute Man Missile purchase program by more than 75 percent; doubled the number of strategic bombers and missiles on alert; doubled the number of nuclear weapons available in the Strategic Alert Forces; increased the tactical nuclear forces deployed in Western Europe by 60 percent; added five combat read divisions and five tactical fighter wings for our Armed Forces; increased our strategic Air Lift capabilities by 75 percent, and increased our special counter-insurgency forces by 600 percent. We can truly say today, with pride in our voices and peace in our hearts, that the defensive forces of the United States are, without a doubt, the most powerful and resourceful forces anywhere in the world.

Finally, I said in Lubbock in 1960, as I said in every other speech in this state, that if Lyndon Johnson and I were elected, we would get this country moving again. That pledge has been fulfilled. In nearly every field of national activity this country is moving again—and Texas is moving with it. From public works to public health, wherever government programs operate, the past three years have shown a new burst of action and progress—in Texas and all over America. We have stepped up the fight against crime and slums and poverty in our cities, against the pollution of our streams, against unemployment in our industry and against waste in the federal government. We have built hospitals, clinics, and nursing homes. We have launched a broad new attack on mental illness and mental retardation. We have initiated the training of more physicians and dentists. We have provided four times as much housing for our elderly citizens—and we have increased benefits for those on social security.

Almost everywhere we look, the story is the same. In Latin America, in Africa, in Asia—in the councils of the world and in the jungles of far-off nations—there is now renewed confidence in our country and our convictions.

This country is moving, and it must not stop. It cannot stop. This is a time for courage and a time of challenge. Neither conformity nor complacency will do. Neither the fanatics nor the faint-hearted are needed. And our duty as a party is not to our party alone, but to the nation, and indeed to all mankind. Our duty is not merely power but the preservation of peace and freedom.

So let us not be petty when our cause is so great. Let us not quarrel amongst ourselves when our nation's future is at stake. Let us stand together with renewed confidence in our case—united in our heritage of the past and our hopes for the future—and determined that this land we love shall lead all mankind into new frontiers of peace and abundance. ✦

Acknowledgments

My thanks are owed to several people for their contributions to this project, but first on the list is Larry King, always a cordial host. His television interview with me on CNN caught the eye of a resourceful literary agent, Bill Adler.

The rest really is history. I needed no help in reliving the events that occurred on that nightmarish day in Dallas, forty years ago. But I am indebted to Julian Read, a longtime friend and former aide to my husband, during his terms as governor of Texas, for helping to guide me through the process.

I feel fortunate to have a publisher, Shawn Coyne, who provided both patience and energy, and a dedicated editor, Chris Min. I'm not sure I should mention anyone's ages. But both were born after the assassination of President Kennedy, giving the book the perspective of another generation.

Three friends were extremely helpful in reinforcing my memories of that confused and tragic time: Nancy Sayers Abington, Adele Locke Seybold, and my sister-in-law, Mary Connally. Larry Temple, like Julian a former member of the governor's staff, was another source of information. I also want to thank Jay Wurts for his editing help.

In a personal and sentimental aside, I believe John Connally would be pleased to know that I was assisted in this work by another family friend, Mickey Herskowitz, who was the co-author of John's autobiography.

Credits